Conveyancing Quali Toolkit

CW00722969

Related titles from Law Society Publishing:

Conveyancing Checklists, 2nd edn
Frances Silverman and Russell Hewitson

Conveyancing Forms and Procedures, 4th edn
Annette Goss, Lorraine Richardson and Michael Taylor

Conveyancing Handbook, 18th edn
General editor: Frances Silverman, Consultant Editors: Annette Goss, Russell Hewitson, Peter Reekie, Anne Rodell and Michael Taylor

Conveyancing Protocol
The Law Society

Environmental Law Handbook, 7th edn
Valerie Fogleman, Trevor Hellawell and Andrew Wiseman

Titles from Law Society Publishing can be ordered from all good bookshops or direct (telephone 0870 850 1422, email **lawsociety@prolog.uk.com** or visit our online shop at **www.lawsociety.org.uk/ bookshop**).

Conveyancing Quality Scheme Toolkit

The Law Society

The Law Society

All rights reserved. The purchaser may reproduce and/or store the contents of the disk that accompanies this publication for the practice's internal practice management purposes only. The publication may not be reproduced in whole or in part for resale or commercial use, or for distribution otherwise to any third parties.

All rights reserved. No part of this publication may be reproduced in any material form, whether by photocopying, scanning, downloading onto computer or otherwise without the written permission of the Law Society except in accordance with the provisions of the Copyright, Designs and Patents Act 1988. Applications should be addressed in the first instance, in writing, to Law Society Publishing. Any unauthorised or restricted act in relation to this publication may result in civil proceedings and/or criminal prosecution.

Whilst all reasonable care has been taken in the preparation of this publication, neither the publisher nor the author can accept any responsibility for any loss occasioned to any person acting or refraining from action as a result of relying upon its contents.

© The Law Society 2011 except 2.15–2.17

© Peter Camp 2011 – 2.15–2.17 only

ISBN-13: 978-1-907698-20-0

Published in 2011 by the Law Society
113 Chancery Lane, London WC2A 1PL

Typeset by Columns Design XML Ltd, Reading
Printed by Hobbs the Printers Ltd, Totton, Hants

The paper used for the text pages of this book is FSC®certified. FSC (the Forest Stewardship Council®) is an international network to promote responsible management of the world's forests.

Contents

Preface		vii
1	**Financial management**	**1**
	1.1 Financial management procedures	3
2	**Supervision and operational risk management**	**9**
	2.1 Management structure of the practice	11
	2.2 Supervision policy	12
	2.3 File review policy	13
	2.4 File summary sheet	14
	2.5 Standard file review – conveyancing purchase	16
	2.6 Standard file review – conveyancing sale	18
	2.7 Policy on risk	19
	2.8 Risk management policy	22
	2.9 Risk management analysis spreadsheet – purchase	24
	2.10 Risk management analysis spreadsheet – sale	27
	2.11 Business continuity planning	29
	2.12 Business continuity – telephone list	32
	2.13 Business continuity – risk matrix	33
	2.14 Mortgage fraud policy	34
	2.15 Anti-money laundering policy	37
	2.16 Anti-money laundering – client identification form	46
	2.17 Anti-money laundering – internal reporting form	49
	2.18 E-mail policy	51

3   **Client care**   **55**

      3.1   Client care policy   57

      3.2   Client care letter – conveyancing   62

      3.3   Closing letter   67

      3.4   Standard terms and conditions of business for
            conveyancing clients   69

      3.5   Client survey   77

      3.6   Clients complaints policy   78

4   **File and case management**   **81**

      4.1   Procedure for acceptance of new matters, allocation of work
            and file management   83

      4.2   Client instruction form   87

      4.3   Policy for the giving of undertakings   91

      4.4   SRA Warning Card on Undertakings   92

      4.5   Risk notice   94

      4.6   File risk assessment and conflict of interests check form   95

Preface

The Law Society Conveyancing Quality Scheme (CQS) accreditation is a mark of excellence for the residential conveyancing market. Law firms of all sizes regulated by the Solicitors Regulation Authority are gaining the new accreditation nationwide. It holds recognition amongst numerous influential stakeholders, including those from the mortgage lending and insurance industries. A firm with CQS will demonstrate strong client care credentials, high practice management standards, deliver quality services and demonstrate a commitment to excellence.

The *Conveyancing Quality Scheme Toolkit* is intended to help your practice comply with and implement some of those qualities through adherence to the core practice management standards. These standards must be followed by all member practices under CQS if they do not already have the documented procedures in place.

The toolkit is practical in nature and aimed at assisting solicitors with their day-to-day responsibilities of practice management. It contains a range of example or template policies, procedures and documents which can be adopted easily but need to be amended to suit your practice's needs. Adoption of the documentation within this toolkit supports compliance with the core practice management standards but does not guarantee compliance with any regulatory requirements.

The toolkit includes a wide range of template documents including:

- risk management policy;
- supervision policy;
- file review policy;
- client care letter;
- client survey;
- policy for the giving of undertakings;
- mortgage fraud policy.

All of these are provided in this book and accompanying free CD-ROM, enabling you to customise them as needed.

We hope that you will find the *Conveyancing Quality Scheme Toolkit* useful both as a reference guide and as a practical resource in your day-to-day work.

This toolkit was compiled by Peter Rodd (Partner at Boys and Maughan Solicitors and Chairman of the Law Society Property Section) with the assistance of Andrew Baker (also a Partner at Boys and Maughan Solicitors) and Clare Jarrett of the Law Society.

Conveyancing Quality Scheme Office
The Law Society

PART 1
Financial management

1.1 Financial management procedures

Responsibility for financial management

All [partners/members/directors] have a responsibility for financial management. [*Name*] has direct responsibility for overall financial management in the practice. In this task [he/she] is supported by other [partners/members/directors] with more specific responsibilities, such as department heads. On a daily basis, much of the control and supervision is delegated to the [*job title*] and the [*name of department*] staff.

Individual fee-earners are responsible for the financial management of their client matters as required by the Solicitors' Accounts Rules and the detailed instructions that follow.

If anyone has cause to be concerned about any aspect of financial management, especially as related to client monies, they should refer their concern to [*name*] or another [partner/member/director].

[Computer system

[*If applicable*]

The practice uses [*name of software*], a centralised accounting and time recording system. All personnel have direct access to much of the system and the data on it through the computer network. The software is provided by [*name of provider*]. If there are any difficulties concerning the system they should be directed to [*main contact within practice*].

Generally, [*specify*] personnel have enquiry access to all client accounting and time recording data, which also allows queries and related printouts to be produced. In addition, [*job title(s) of roles with management responsibilities*] have access to specific management reporting facilities. Apart from time recording entries, only the [*job title(s)*] and [*name of department*] personnel have password-protected access to the various posting programs.

All staff are encouraged to use the accounting information available to support their client work but should refer to [*name of department*] personnel if specific help is required.]

Management reports

Management reports are produced [*frequency*] by the [*name of department*]. The Conveyancing Quality Scheme (CQS) Senior Responsible Officer (SRO), [*senior finance job title*] and staff with responsibility for overall management of [*practice name*] have specific responsibility for reviewing such reports.

Regular review of management reports

Every [*month*] [*name of accountants appointed by the practice*] produce annual accounts which include:

* profit and loss account
* balance sheet.

These are certified/audited, then distributed to and reviewed by [*job title(s)*].

At the beginning of each financial year the [*job title*] will produce an annual budget and cash flow projections as part of the business planning process. Responsibilities for delivering against budget reside with [*job title(s)*].

Every [month/two months/quarter] the following reports will be produced by the practice:

* profit and loss account
* balance sheet
* budget variance report
* report showing variance of actual cash flow against projected cash flow
* [*any other reports which are distributed regularly*].

These are distributed to and reviewed by [*job title(s)*].

Other reports can be produced on request to the [*job title/department*] with consent from [*job title*].

Income and expenditure budgets

Budgets are an essential tool in the financial management of any practice. They provide an opportunity to outline our plans for the coming year, which can then be measured against actual results. Annual income and expenditure budgets are prepared at a practice level and a department level. These are used to monitor the practice's financial performance, as well as each department's financial performance. Every [month/two months/quarter] the [*job title(s)*] review(s) budget variance reports.

Cash flow

Based largely on known or anticipated income and expenditure budgets, a cash flow forecast for the forthcoming year is prepared by [*name of individual/ department*]. The cash flow forecast is kept under continual review and forms part of the [monthly/two-monthly/quarterly] management review.

Cash flow is managed largely at practice level. It is important, however, that all fee-earners remain alert to the need for them to manage their own client matters carefully. Fee-earners should ensure, where possible, money on account of disbursements (where applicable) is obtained. Final bills need to be raised promptly and the fee-earner needs to remain involved in any credit control action.

Receipt of cash and cheques

Most monies are received by cheque or by electronic transfer, but payment in cash is sometimes offered. [*Practice name*]'s policy on receiving cash is influenced by its responsibilities under money laundering legislation (see the anti-money laundering policy at **2.15**).

Cash

[*Practice name*] will not accept cash of more than £[*amount*] per transaction. This is due to money laundering regulations, the responsibilities of staff taking the money to the bank, and our insurance cover for holding cash being for amounts of no more than £[*amount*].

If a sum of cash is received it should be counted initially by the fee-earner or receptionist receiving it. It must then be taken across personally to the [*name of department*] where the [*job title*] will count it and arrange for it to be banked. All cash should be held in the practice's safe until banked.

Payments of large amounts should always be made by direct bank transfer (BACS or CHAPS). Payments of amounts over £[*amount*] should always be refused due to the money laundering implications.

Cash is never to be left unattended, for example, left out on a desk.

Cheques

Cheques received in the morning post must be sent direct to [*name of department*] without delay in order that they can be safeguarded, identified and banked on the same day. Cheques received later in the day or direct by a fee-earner must also be sent to [*name of department*] without delay, even if they cannot be banked on that day.

All cheques must be banked without delay, which means, in normal circumstances, on the day of receipt or the next working day, in accordance with the Solicitors' Accounts Rules, rule 2(1)(z).

On receipt of any cheque, as with all payments, [*set out practice's procedures for payments in*].

[*Name of department*] cannot accept any monies in unless the correct procedure is followed.

Cheque requisitions

If a fee-earner requires a cheque to be drawn on a client account or an office account, the fee-earner is to [*set out procedures for requisitioning a cheque*].

[*Name of department*] will make the assumption that cheques will be issued on that day if the funds are cleared and will effect the ledger posting accordingly. If the issue of the cheque is to be delayed, then the fee-earner must make this clear and liaise with [*name of department*].

Transfers

[*Set out procedure for transfers between client ledgers.*]

On occasions it may be necessary to support the transfer form with a note of explanation.

The proper transferring of monies is directly the responsibility of fee-earners and verbal instructions will not be accepted by [*name of department*].

CHAPS transfers

[*Set out procedures for requesting a telegraphic transfer.*]

BACS transfers

[*Set out procedures for requesting a BACS transfer.*]

Payment out of client monies

Payment out of client monies by cheque or transfer, irrespective of the amount, can be authorised only by a [partner/member/director], assistant solicitor or FILEX member by [*set out procedures for authorising payments out in accordance with the Solicitors' Accounts Rules*].

Cheques can be signed only by [a/two] [partner(s)/member(s)/director(s)] in accordance with the bank mandate.

Write-offs

Office balances

The write-off of any balance in respect of costs or disbursements can be authorised only by a [partner/member/director]. [*Set out procedures for authorising office account write-offs.*]

Client balances

In exceptional cases it may be desirable to write off a balance of client monies where, despite all endeavours, it has not been possible to trace the client.

Prior to 14 July 2008, it was necessary to apply to the Solicitors Regulation Authority (SRA) for authority to pay such balances to a charity. After 14 July 2008, under the Solicitors' Accounts (Residual Client Account Balances) Amendment Rules 2008, any amounts under £50 can be donated to a charity provided that the practice has complied with rule 22(2A) of the Solicitors' Accounts Rules.

Rule 22(2A) provides that a practice can withdraw such money provided that it:

  (a) establishes the identity of the owner of the money, or makes reasonable attempts to do so;
  (b) makes adequate attempts to ascertain the proper destination of the money, and to return it to the rightful owner, unless the reasonable costs of doing so are likely to be excessive in relation to the amount held;
  (c) pays the funds to a charity; ...

Under rule 22(2A)(e), we are required to keep a central register of all account balances paid to charity.

For amounts of over £50, an application will need to be made to the SRA for written authority to withdraw the money. The SRA may impose a condition that the money is paid to a charity which gives an indemnity against any legitimate claim subsequently made for the sum received.

Petty cash

[*Set out procedures for the holding and use of petty cash.*]

Issue of bills

[*Set out procedures for issue of bills.*]

Receipt of funds from third parties

[Set out procedures for receipt of funds from third parties.]

PART 2

Supervision and operational risk management

2.1 Management structure of the practice

[*Practice name*] is a [partnership/LLP/limited company] whose head office is at [*head office address*].

The members of the senior management team with overall responsibility for the practice are:

- [*list members of senior management team including name, job title and office location*].

The person in overall charge of conveyancing at [*practice name*] is [*name and job title*]. [*Name and job title*] is the Senior Responsible Officer (SRO) for the purpose of the Conveyancing Quality Standard (CQS). CQS is the optional accreditation scheme [*practice name*] has sought and achieved accreditation in. We are committed to maintaining our accreditation which was awarded on [*date*].

[*Name*] is responsible for all conveyancing at the practice and also for maintenance of appropriate supervision and risk management procedures within the practice. [He/she] is also responsible for the maintenance of the CQS Core Practice Management Standards. These standards must be embedded throughout the conveyancing department to help us follow best practice principles.

[*For use where there is more than one department*:]

[*Name*] is assisted in the above by [*job titles, e.g.* the department heads] who are responsible for supervision, risk management and maintenance of the CQS Core Practice Management Standards within their department.

The departments are as follows:

[*Head of Department 1*]	[*Team member*]
	[*Team member*]
	[*Team member*]
[*Head of Department 2*]	[*Team member*]
	[*Team member*]
	[*Team member*]
[*Head of Department 3*]	[*Team member*]
	[*Team member*]
	[*Team member*]

2.2 Supervision policy

Supervision is effected by:

- The allocation of all work to the appropriate fee-earner/department.
- Spot checks on incoming post by [*job title*] in the conveyancing department at least [*frequency and volume*].
- All inexperienced fee-earners having to copy letters, e-mails or text messages of any substantive advice to their immediate supervisor at the time the letter is created.
- All contract reports prepared by inexperienced fee-earners being checked by a [*job title*].
- Departmental meetings held [*frequency*], when technical problems can be discussed.
- Regular file reviews and audits carried out at least [*frequency*].
- Regular checks on fee-earner workloads to ensure that no fee-earner exceeds [*number*] matters and in general average workloads are kept to [*number*] matters at any one time.
- An open-door policy at all times for all those in a supervisory role.

2.3 File review policy

[*Practice name*] operates a system of regular, independent file reviews. A central record of file reviews is kept by [*name*], the [head of the conveyancing department/ SRO]. A copy of all reviews should be sent to [him/her] within [*timeframe*].

The [head of conveyancing/SRO] will arrange for file reviews to be carried out on a quarterly basis. The selection of files should be generated from a list of matters for each conveyancer. A different focus of review may be adopted from time to time but it is important that at least one file should be of a recently archived matter to ensure that all aspects of the conveyancing procedure have been carried out in accordance with the practice's policy.

A file review sheet (see **2.5** and **2.6**) will be completed when any such independent file review occurs. Copies will be put on to the matter file and on to a central departmental list of all review sheets to verify that reviews are occurring as planned and that any corrective action identified as being necessary is being taken. When corrective action is required, it is the responsibility of the conveyancer to undertake the corrective action specified within the time period specified, and in no case will this be longer than 28 days. The reviewer must then verify to his or her reasonable satisfaction that the corrective action has been performed and sign and date the review form to show that the corrective action has been taken within 28 days.

It is the responsibility of the SRO to review all file review data at least annually and include an analysis of and recommendations based on the file review data in the annual review of the operation of the quality management system.

Where it is apparent that a trend exists (e.g. one conveyancer regularly 'failing' in one area or another, or several conveyancers 'failing' in one particular area) the SRO should arrange for appropriate additional training to be given.

As a minimum, three files per quarter should be reviewed for all fee-earners. Two files should be for purchase matters and one for a sale matter. Where the practice undertakes remortgage work, an additional file should be reviewed for a remortgage transaction each quarter.

2.4 File summary sheet

Client name		Date file opened	
Fee-earner		Matter number	

Initial risk assessment

Ordinary risk ☐

Referred to risk manager ☐

Beginning of the matter

Procedure	Action	Date
Client objectives recorded		
Client identification verified		
Conflict of interest check		
Case plan completed		
Method of funding established and cost benefit analysis conducted		
Key dates recorded on file and in back-up system		
Client engagement letter issued		

During the matter

Procedure	Action	Date
Client notified of change in fee-earner/ supervisor		
Conflict of interest check		
Client updated on costs		
Client informed of adverse costs order		
Undertaking given		
Barrister or other service provider instructed		
Complaints procedure forwarded to client		

Interim risk assessment

Change in risk profile? Yes ☐ No ☐ Referred to risk manager ☐

End of the matter

Procedure	Action	Date
Client notified of outcome		
Client accounted to for any outstanding money		
Original documents returned to client		
Original documents retained on behalf of client		
Client advised on storage and retrieval of papers		
Client advised of matter review process		

Concluding risk assessment

Client objectives achieved?   Yes ☐   No ☐   Referred to risk manager ☐

2.5 Standard file review – conveyancing purchase

Client name		Account number	
Fee-earner		Department	
Date of review		Reviewer	

Check for:	Yes	No	N/A	Action required
Evidence of ID				
Evidence of source of funds				
Written quote/estimate of costs and disbursements				
Terms and conditions signed by all parties				
Money received on account				
Mortgage lender advised as to ID of other conveyancer (where required)				
Contract report sent/correct advice given				
Correct copy documents on file				
Correct searches on file				
Any non-standard undertakings given				
Transaction dealt with expeditiously				
No delay in SDLT submission				
No delay in application for registration				
Registration within priority period				
Prompt report of registration to client and mortgage lender				
Apparent breaches of CQS protocol				

Comments/corrective action required
Long term action/training identified
Action taken by fee-earner (must be taken within 28 days)
Signed
Date
Action verified by reviewer
Signed
Date

2.6 Standard file review – conveyancing sale

Client name		Account number	
Fee-earner		Department	
Date of review		Reviewer	

Check for:	Yes	No	N/A	Action required
Sub files used				
Evidence of ID				
Terms and conditions signed				
Written quote (on inside cover of file)				
Complete documentation supplied or explanation given				
Correct searches on file				
Correct copy documents on file				
Any non-standard undertakings given				
Transaction dealt with expeditiously				
Apparent breaches of CQS protocol				
Proceeds of sale to clients				

Comments/corrective action required
Long term action/training identified
Action taken by fee-earner (must be taken within 28 days)
Signed
Date
Action verified by reviewer
Signed
Date

2.7 Policy on risk

Reporting risk

Risk is an issue before, during and after action is taken in every matter. The proactive management of risk issues will reduce the incidence of claims and complaints in most practices. The level of risk presented by every file needs to be considered by [*job title(s)*].

Before

Before acting, a fee-earner must make an initial risk assessment as part of the file opening procedures. The fee-earner must determine whether the matter is 'low', 'medium' or 'high' risk. Most matters will be low risk, i.e. present no risks other than those arising out of day-to-day practice.

Matters should be considered medium risk if they present risks to the practice over and above day-to-day risks, but these risks are standard risks of the practice areas which are dealt with by procedures put in place to prevent the risk becoming a complaint or claim.

A matter should be judged to be high risk if:

- There is a novel or unusual aspect of law involved.
- A foreign jurisdiction may be involved.
- The consideration is very high. Note that the maximum sum payable under the practice's insurance policy for any one claim is £[*amount*] million. Any matter where the value of the matter or potential consequence of a mistake could exceed this should be reported to the practice's senior management team before the matter is taken on.
- The client has transferred this matter to the practice in circumstances where they were dissatisfied with the advice or service provided by their previous advisers.
- Several money laundering or mortgage fraud warning signs are present.

All high-risk assessments must be brought to the attention of the [risk partner/head of department] when the file is opened. They can then review whether the practice should accept these instructions and, if so, what precautionary steps in relation to responsibility, supervision and review should be imposed.

During

During a matter, its risk profile could change at any time. This might involve greater risk to the practice or the client. A change of circumstances so far as the client is concerned will need to be raised with the client: if there is any suggestion that the practice could be at risk from the changed circumstances, especially if the accuracy or appropriateness of advice to date could now be questioned, a risk notice must be completed on the risk notice form (see **4.5**) and forwarded to the appropriate head of department with a copy to the risk manager without delay.

After

After a matter is finished there needs to be a concluding risk assessment, which is noted on the file closing sheet. If it is considered that the practice should have done better for a client and that they could fairly complain about the service provided or make a claim, the fee-earner must complete a risk notice on the risk notice form (see **4.5**) and forward it to the appropriate head of department with a copy to the risk manager. On receipt of such a notice, a view will have to be taken as to whether the practice is required under the terms of its indemnity insurance contract to make a report.

In summary, if you have a concern before, during or after any matter, share it with your colleagues and make sure that it is reported if there could be a complaint or a claim.

Responsibility for risk management

The fees for the practice's annual indemnity insurance represent a considerable item of expenditure for the practice and are geared very heavily to its risk profile, which in turn is judged largely on its claims record. In any event, if the practice is committed to providing the best legal advice possible, it needs to consider its responsibilities to clients to avoid the loss, inconvenience and harm to its reputation that could arise from its negligence.

[*Practice name*] accepts that it cannot possibly operate a 'risk-free' practice. It is important, however, that the practice takes all reasonable steps to minimise the risk of a claim or a complaint against it. This has to involve all personnel.

The main thrust of the practice's risk management policy is that prevention is better than a cure. The risk manager is responsible for the management of the practice's risk profile. In this respect [he/she] will:

- continually review the practice's policy, procedures and arrangements for the management of risk and submit an annual report on risk management to the senior management team;
- every six months, discuss issues of concern with the senior management team;

- receive risk reports on the risk notice form and take appropriate action in respect of them;
- monitor new aspects of risk that could develop and report these accordingly to the senior management team;
- negotiate and liaise with the practice's professional indemnity insurers/ brokers;
- take whatever action seems appropriate to ensure that risk is identified, anticipated and guarded against, so far as possible;
- arrange training on risk issues if appropriate.

2.8 Risk management policy

Commitment

[*Practice name*] is committed to sound corporate governance and has made risk management an integral part of its strategic planning and review processes. Risk management will be highlighted in induction and will underpin all practice management procedures.

Scope

The scope of this policy embraces all permanent and temporary employees, and systems or processes for the identification, control and monitoring of risks. We cover the following categories:

- Strategic risk
- Operational risk
- Regulatory risk

Approach

The practice has initiated a systematic approach to the management of risk including:

- compiling a risk register;
- compiling a risk management action plan;
- maintaining a list of work that the practice will and will not undertake;
- conducting an annual review of complaints data;
- providing staff briefing and training on risk identification, control and reporting.

Responsibilities

Risk manager

The designated risk manager for the practice is [*name*]. He/she has overall responsibility for risk management in the practice.

Senior management team

The senior management team is responsible for determining the strategic direction of the practice and for carrying out strategic risk reviews. It is also responsible for creating the culture and environment for risk management to operate effectively throughout the practice.

Supervisors

Supervisors have primary responsibility for managing risk on a day-to-day basis. They are also responsible for promoting risk awareness within their teams.

Staff

All staff have a responsibility for identifying, controlling and reporting risk at a level appropriate to their role. In order to facilitate this, all staff are required to keep up to date with the procedures outlined in the office manual.

Review

In order to ensure that it remains fit for purpose, this policy will be formally reviewed at least annually by the senior management team. This review process will also serve as a means of continually improving the practice's approach to risk management.

Signed:

[*Name*], Risk Manager

Date:

2.9 Risk management analysis spreadsheet – purchase

First quarter	FE	FE	FE	FE	FE	FE	Totals
Evidence of ID.							
Evidence of source of funds							
Written quote/estimate of costs and disbursements							
Terms and conditions signed by all parties							
Money received on account							
Mortgage lender advised as to ID of other conveyancer (where required)							
Contract report sent/correct advice given							
Correct copy documents on file							
Correct searches on file							
Any non-standard undertakings given							
Transaction dealt with expeditiously							
No delay in SDLT submission							
No delay in application for registration							
Registration within priority period							
Prompt report of registration to client and mortgage lender							
Apparent breaches of CQS protocol							

Second quarter	FE	FE	FE	FE	FE	FE	Totals
Evidence of ID							
Evidence of source of funds							
Written quote/estimate of costs and disbursements							
Terms and conditions signed by all parties							
Money received on account							
Mortgage lender advised as to ID of other conveyancer (where required)							

Second quarter	FE	FE	FE	FE	FE	FE	Totals
Contract report sent/correct advice given							
Correct copy documents on file							
Correct searches on file							
Any non-standard undertakings given							
Transaction dealt with expeditiously							
No delay in SDLT submission							
No delay in application for registration							
Registration within priority period							
Prompt report of registration to client and mortgage lender							
Apparent breaches of CQS protocol							

Third quarter	FE	FE	FE	FE	FE	FE	Totals
Evidence of ID							
Evidence of source of funds							
Written quote/estimate of costs and disbursements							
Terms and conditions signed by all parties							
Money received on account							
Mortgage lender advised as to ID of other conveyancer (where required)							
Contract report sent/correct advice given							
Correct copy documents on file							
Correct searches on file							
Any non-standard undertakings given							
Transaction dealt with expeditiously							
No delay in SDLT submission							
No delay in application for registration							
Registration within priority period							
Prompt report of registration to client and mortgage lender							
Apparent breaches of CQS protocol							

Fourth quarter	FE	FE	FE	FE	FE	FE	Totals
Evidence of ID							
Evidence of source of funds							
Written quote/estimate of costs and disbursements							
Terms and conditions signed by all parties							
Money received on account							
Mortgage lender advised as to ID of other conveyancer (where required)							
Contract report sent/correct advice given							
Correct copy documents on file							
Correct searches on file							
Any non-standard undertakings given							
Transaction dealt with expeditiously							
No delay in SDLT submission							
No delay in application for registration							
Registration within priority period							
Prompt report of registration to client and mortgage lender							
Apparent breaches of CQS protocol							

Totals							

2.10 Risk management analysis spreadsheet – sale

First quarter	FE	FE	FE	FE	FE	FE	Totals
Sub files used							
Evidence of ID							
Terms and conditions signed							
Written quote (on inside cover of file)							
Complete documentation supplied or explanation given							
Correct searches on file							
Correct copy documents on file							
Any non-standard undertakings given							
Transaction dealt with expeditiously							
Apparent breaches of CQS protocol							
Proceeds of sale to clients							

Second quarter	FE	FE	FE	FE	FE	FE	Totals
Sub files used							
Evidence of ID							
Terms and conditions signed							
Written quote (on inside cover of file)							
Complete documentation supplied or explanation given							
Correct searches on file							
Correct copy documents on file							
Any non-standard undertakings given							
Transaction dealt with expeditiously							
Apparent breaches of CQS protocol							
Proceeds of sale to clients							

Third quarter	FE	FE	FE	FE	FE	FE	Totals
Sub files used							
Evidence of ID							
Terms and conditions signed							
Written quote (on inside cover of file)							
Complete documentation supplied or explanation given							
Correct searches on file							
Correct copy documents on file							
Any non-standard undertakings given							
Transaction dealt with expeditiously							
Apparent breaches of CQS protocol							
Proceeds of sale to clients							

Fourth quarter	FE	FE	FE	FE	FE	FE	Totals
Sub files used							
Evidence of ID							
Terms and conditions signed							
Written quote (on inside cover of file)							
Complete documentation supplied or explanation given							
Correct searches on file							
Correct copy documents on file							
Any non-standard undertakings given							
Transaction dealt with expeditiously							
Apparent breaches of CQS protocol							
Proceeds of sale to clients							

Totals							

2.11 Business continuity planning

Introduction

Business continuity might be something of an alien subject. In many conveyancing practices, staff may find it difficult to have the time or motivation to pay much attention to it. It has, however, been a part of the Solicitors' Code of Conduct since 2007, and has other benefits to any business serving the general public.

Pressures for business continuity

Conveyancing practices are organisations on which clients depend, and client expectations are high. These high expectations also include the clients' perception that the practice will always be available to deal with their matters, hence the need for good business continuity plans. This is echoed in a raft of regulatory advice and requirements, including the Solicitors' Code of Conduct.

Naturally, one cannot ignore the fact that a practice is a commercial concern. Therefore, the speedy resumption of business that is facilitated by a good business continuity plan not only ensures ongoing profitability, but also has the potential to enhance the reputation of the practice.

Additionally, practices deal with highly regulated clients such as banks, financial institutions and ordinary companies. Often clients will reflect their own regulatory pressures on their suppliers of services. Increasingly, tenders require formal reassurance as to the continuity plans of their suppliers, even to the point of requiring sight of a practice's continuity plan.

CQS requirements

The CQS Core Practice Management Standards state:

1.4 Practices will have a business continuity plan, which must include:

    a: an evaluation of potential threats and the likelihood of their impact
    b: ways to reduce, avoid and transfer the risk
    c: processes for testing and checking the plan
    d: the person responsible for the plan
    e: a procedure to test the plan annually, to verify that it would be effective in the event of a business interruption.

Resources

The business continuity plan will need to be appropriate for your conveyancing practice. The pressures on a small practice are going to be very different from those with large multi-site operations. There is no point in a business continuity plan that uses so much of your practice's resources (time and money) that it impacts in a negative way on your day-to-day work. Often practices will find out that they are already providing for business continuity and it is just a case of setting out the procedures in the plan then taking them a stage further to ensure that risks are dealt with proportionately and appropriately.

For larger practices, detailed guidance on business continuity planning, including a planning template, may be found in the *Lexcel Business Continuity Planning Toolkit* (Law Society, 2011).

Here are some of the risks that all practices may want to consider:

Fire

- Who is responsible for your fire management processes/policies?
- What problems would arise if there was a fire while people were in the building?
- What is the frequency and effectiveness of any fire drills and evacuation plans?
- What would happen if there was a fire while the office was closed?
- How would the practice restart business?
- How would the practice communicate with staff and clients?
- Does the practice have alternative premises to use in the event of a fire damaging the office?

Flood

- How likely is the risk of a flood?
- What would the practice do about IT systems in the event of a flood?
- What would the practice do about recovery of hard-copy documents?
- Does the threat of flood affect where any information assets are stored?

IT

- All conveyancing practices will be dependent on IT in one way or another. For example, what would happen if communications to banks were interrupted, making CHAPS payments impossible?
- What back-ups of the IT data does the practice undertake?
- Where are back-ups stored? Are they taken off site to a secure location?
- What would happen in the event of a power interruption? Would the computers safely shut down without destroying any data?

- If the power interruption were more than a temporary disruption, what would the practice do?

Personnel

- What would happen if a key member of staff were incapacitated for a period of time, for example, on long term sick leave? Is there anyone with sufficient knowledge to be able to fill in for them?
- What would the practice do in the event of a flu pandemic? What plans does the practice have in place in case a flu pandemic occurs, both to protect those at work and to cover for those who are off work?

Communication

- How would the practice communicate with staff and clients in the event of a communications breakdown, for example, a sustained loss of the practice's telephone system?
- How would the practice communicate with staff and clients in the event of a closure of the main office because of fire or some other eventuality?
- How would the practice deal with a key member of staff getting into trouble or being arrested to prevent reputational damage (which could do as much damage as any physical disaster)?

What to do with a business continuity plan

A business continuity plan that once finished is locked away and forgotten about is a waste of all the resources invested in it. It is important that all staff are aware of it and the relevant parts are communicated to those staff who need to know. The plan will need to be reviewed at least annually and updated, with any changes being communicated to everyone.

Testing the plan

The CQS Core Practice Management Standards require that there is a procedure for testing the plan at least annually to verify that it is effective in operation across the practice.

Ways of testing the plan can include:

- fire drills, which should be a regular feature of testing the plan;
- implementing the telephone cascade system;
- testing the IT back-up to ensure it is effective and shuts down safely;
- switching to alternative banking facilities;
- testing alternative communication systems.

2.12 Business continuity – telephone list

In the event of an emergency where communications are not possible through usual means, the senior management team will communicate with everyone through the department heads using the contact numbers below. The department heads will communicate with everyone in their group as denoted by group letter.

Name	Job description	Telephone numbers			Group	Remarks
		Office	Mobile	Home		
					All	Senior management team
					All	
					All	
					A	Department heads
					B	
					C	
					A	Team members
					A	
					A	
					A	
					A	
					B	
					B	
					B	
					B	
					B	
					C	
					C	
					C	
					C	

2.13 Business continuity – risk matrix

Type of disruption	Duration of loss/time-frame	Disruption to work	Financial loss	Client impact	Damage to reputation	Regulatory issues	Steps taken to minimise disruption or risk of disruption	Recovery Time Objective (RTO)	Recovery Point Objective (RPO)
Examples									
Small contained fire in main office building	1 day	Significant	2 hours loss of work for affected department	Loss of communication to affected department for 2 hours	Small if communications contained	Limited	• Fire drills practised every 6 months • Two back-up computers kept in case needed (located in store) • Communications to be by mobiles to department heads using telephone cascade system whilst building is evacuated	2 hours	All fee-earners back at work stations and continuing work
Large fire rendering main office unusable for several weeks	6 weeks	Very severe	Substantial (refer to insurance policy for extent of cover)	Could be very severe if not able to operate at an alternative site within a few hours	Could be very severe if not able to operate at an alternative site within a few hours	Need to ensure that alternative site is available which allows compliance with regulatory requirements	• Senior management to meet and decide plan for continuing business • Communication by mobiles to department heads using telephone cascade system • Alternative location to be agreed by senior management team using remote back-up from [*name of computer hardware/software provider*]	• Communications with clients restored within 3 hours • Temporary site up and running within 1 day. • Full service restored at temporary site within 5 working days • Relocation back to permanent site within 6 weeks	Back at permanent site within 6 weeks

2.14 Mortgage fraud policy

It is possible that a member of staff may unwittingly assist in a mortgage fraud. This is especially true of staff who deal with any form of conveyancing, whether domestic or commercial. [*Practice name*] must therefore be very vigilant to protect mortgagee clients and itself. If you turn a blind eye to any form of dishonesty over mortgages, no matter how small, you too could be personally implicated in the fraud.

No matter how much you want to help your client, you must not be a party to any form of dishonesty. Giving false information on the mortgage application, e.g. with respect to income, employment or other financial commitments, means that the mortgage is being obtained fraudulently. When that mortgage is drawn down the advance may be considered to be the proceeds of crime and subject to anti-money laundering (AML) regulations.

Could you spot a mortgage fraud? The signs to watch for are:

- Fictitious buyer – especially if the buyer is introduced to the practice by a third party (e.g. a broker or estate agent) who is not well known to you. Beware of clients whom you never meet – they may be fictitious. Remember that if we do not meet the client, the AML regulations require us to carry out enhanced due diligence.
- Unusual instructions – for example, if you are instructed to remit the net proceeds of sale to the estate agent who was instructed or indeed any other third party. We should only ever pay any mortgages or other charges secured on the property and then account to the client for the net proceeds of sale. Never be tempted to try and 'help out' the client by sending money overseas 'to pay a deposit on a villa or boat'.
- Misrepresentation of the purchase price – make sure that the true cash price for a property which is to be actually paid is the price shown in the contract and the transfer, and is identical to the price shown in the mortgage instructions. Remember the requirements of the CML handbook or BSA instructions with regard to buyer incentives, especially when provided by a developer. Always ensure that the incentives declaration form is completed: **www.cml.org.uk/cml/ handbook/form**.
- A deposit paid direct – a deposit, perhaps exceeding the normal 10 per cent, paid direct, or said to be direct, to the seller.
- Incomplete contract documentation – contract documents not fully completed by the seller's representative, i.e. dates missing or the identity of the parties not fully described.
- Changes in the purchase price – adjustments to the purchase price, particularly in high percentage mortgage cases, or allowances off the purchase price for, e.g. works to be carried out.

- Unusual transactions – those which do not follow their normal course or the usual pattern of events. If the transaction is one with which you are not familiar, seek advice from a conveyancing partner.
- Has the property been owned by the current owner for less than six months? Remember your obligations under the CML handbook or BSA instructions even if you are satisfied that there is no possibility of mortgage fraud.
- Has the value of the property significantly increased in a short period of time?
- Does the client usually engage in property investment of this scale?
- Does the client seem unusually uninterested in their purchase?

What steps can you take to minimise the risk of fraud? Be vigilant, if you have any doubts about a transaction, consider whether any part of the following steps could be taken to minimise the risk:

- Verify the identity and bona fides of your client – meet the client or clients where possible and get to know them.
- Relying on other professionals – if you asked to use the reliance provisions in the Money Laundering Regulations 2007 to minimise client due diligence activities, consider whom you are relying upon.

  - Are they regulated for anti-money laundering purposes?
  - Do you know them personally?
  - Are they from an established firm?
  - What is their reputation?
  - Are they able to provide you with the client due diligence material they have?

  Even if you rely on someone else, you are still responsible for ensuring due diligence has been appropriately conducted.

- Question unusual instructions – make sure that you discuss them fully with your client.
- Discuss any aspects of the transaction which worry you with your client – for example, if you suspect that your client may have submitted a false mortgage application or references, or if the lender's valuation exceeds the actual price paid, discuss this with your client and, if you believe they intend to proceed with a fraudulent application, you must refuse to continue to act for the buyer and the mortgagee.
- Check that the true price is shown in all documentation – check that the actual price paid is stated in the contract, transfer and mortgage instructions.
- Ensure that your client understands that, where you are also acting for the lender, you will have to report all allowances and incentives to the mortgagee.
- Do not witness pre-signed documentation – no deed should be witnessed by a solicitor or staff member unless the person signing does so in the presence of a witness. If a deed is pre-signed, ensure that it is re-signed in the presence of a witness.
- Verify signatures – consider whether signatures on all documents connected with a transaction should be examined and compared with signatures on any other documentation, e.g. the client's passport.

- Make a company search – where a private company is the seller or the seller has purchased from a private company in the recent past and you suspect that there may be a connection between the company and the seller or the buyer which is being used for improper purposes, then consideration should be given to making a search in the company's register to ascertain the names and addresses of the offices and shareholders which can then be compared with the names of those connected with the transaction and the seller and buyer.

Mortgage fraud warning

Remember that even where investigations result in a solicitor ceasing to act for a client, the solicitor will still owe a duty of confidentiality which would prevent the solicitor passing on information to the lender. It is only where the solicitor is satisfied that there is a strong prima facie case that the client was using him or her to further a criminal purpose or fraud that the duty of confidentiality would not apply.

Any failure to observe these signs and to take the appropriate steps may be used in evidence against you if you and your client are prosecuted, or if you are sued for negligence.

Money laundering

Strict rules have been introduced, some of which override client confidentiality. Speak to a senior conveyancing partner, the practice's Senior Responsible Officer (SRO) or Money Laundering Reporting Officer (MLRO).

For further guidance see:

- The Law Society's practice notes on:

    - Anti-money laundering: **www.lawsociety.org.uk/productsandservices/ practicenotes/aml.page**
    - Mortgage fraud: **www.lawsociety.org.uk/productsandservices/ practicenotes/mortgagefraud.page**
    - Property and registration fraud: **www.lawsociety.org.uk/ productsandservices/practicenotes/propertyfraud.page**

- CML Lenders' Handbook: **www.cml.org.uk/cml/handbook**
- BSA Mortgage Instructions: **www.bsa.org.uk/mortgageinstructions/index.htm**

2.15 Anti-money laundering policy

What is money laundering?

Money laundering is the process by which the identity of 'dirty money' is changed so that the proceeds of crime appear to originate from a legitimate source. It is important that solicitors and their employees take steps to ensure that their services are not used by those seeking to legitimise the proceeds of crime. Solicitors must be aware that they may be involved in the money laundering process.

It is the policy of [*practice name*] that we will take no avoidable risks and will co-operate fully with the authorities where necessary. No matter how much we want to help our client, we must not be a party to any form of dishonesty. We must be alert to the possibility that transactions on which we are instructed may involve money laundering.

The practice's policy

Legislation (in particular the Proceeds of Crime Act 2002, the Serious Organised Crime and Police Act 2005 and the Money Laundering Regulations 2007) has formalised our responsibilities relating to money laundering. These responsibilities are reflected in this policy.

The criminal offences

The law relating to money laundering changed in February 2003 as a result of the Proceeds of Crime Act 2002. Amendments were introduced by the Serious Organised Crime and Police Act 2005. These amendments were brought into force at various dates in 2005 and 2006. The Money Laundering Regulations 2007 came into force on 15 December 2007. There are a number of criminal offences relevant to a solicitor's practice. The offences divide into three categories:

1. Offences where the practice is involved in a client matter or transaction

It is an offence:

(a) to acquire, use or possess criminal property;
(b) to conceal, disguise, convert, transfer or remove from the UK criminal property; or

(c)   to enter into or become concerned in an arrangement which facilitates the acquisition, retention, use or control of another person's criminal property, in all cases where we know or suspect that this is the case.

Criminal property is defined as constituting or representing a person's benefit from criminal conduct. Criminal conduct for these purposes means any conduct which constitutes a crime in the UK or, if undertaken abroad, would have constituted a crime if committed in the UK.

A defence is available where you disclose your knowledge or suspicion to a nominated officer (i.e. a person nominated by the practice to receive internal disclosures).

The practice's nominated officer is [name]. In [his/her] absence, disclosure should be made to [name of deputy nominated officer].

If you have any knowledge or suspicion which requires reporting, you may initially discuss your concerns with [your supervising partner/the nominated officer]. If after such discussion you still have concerns, a formal disclosure report should be made to the nominated officer using the internal reporting form.

Note that any disclosure you make must generally be made before the prohibited act (i.e. the act of facilitation or otherwise). If you only become aware of information giving rise to knowledge or suspicion whilst committing the prohibited act (for example, you may have placed money in a client account innocently and thereafter discover information which makes you suspicious) you must make your disclosure as soon as possible after you become suspicious. If the disclosure is made after you have committed the prohibited act you will only have a defence if you can show that there was a good reason for your failure to make the disclosure before the act.

(A similar offence relating to the laundering of 'terrorist property' appears in the Terrorism Act 2000.)

A formal disclosure report should be made to the nominated officer using the internal reporting form (see **2.17**).

2. Offences following a disclosure report made to the practice's nominated officer

It is an offence to disclose to any person (including our client) that a report has been made to the practice's nominated officer in circumstances where this is likely to prejudice an investigation. (Further, even if no disclosure report has been made, an offence is committed if you know or suspect that a money laundering investigation is or is likely to be conducted and you disclose any information which is likely to prejudice the investigation.)

Once a report has been made to the nominated officer, it may be an offence to continue to act for the client without the consent of the nominated officer. The nominated officer can only give consent if [he/she] has disclosed details to the Serious Organised Crime Agency (SOCA) and SOCA have, in turn, given consent for the practice to continue to act.

Consequently, once a disclosure has been made to the nominated officer, [he/she] must be involved in every decision relating to that client matter and you must not communicate any information concerning the subject matter of the disclosure to the client or to any other person (including your work colleagues) without the express consent of the nominated officer. Failure to comply with this procedure could lead to a criminal offence being committed.

3. Offences involving a failure to disclose knowledge or suspicion of money laundering

It is an offence for a person who knows or suspects or who has reasonable grounds for knowing or suspecting that another is engaged in money laundering not to disclose that information where the information came to him or her in the course of business in the regulated sector.

The disclosure should be made to the practice's nominated officer using the same procedures as noted above.

This offence does not require the practice to be acting for a particular client, nor for the practice to be in possession, etc. of criminal property, nor involved in an arrangement which facilitates the acquisition, retention, use or control of criminal property.

Further, the offence is not limited to knowledge or suspicion of our client – it applies to any knowledge or suspicion of money laundering offences committed by any person.

The obligation to report arises simply if the information comes into your possession in the course of our business in the regulated sector. The definition of the regulated sector has been extended significantly. The sector now covers the bulk of our work for clients. Consequently, it is [*practice name*]'s policy to assume that all client work falls within the regulated sector and that accordingly all knowledge or suspicion of money laundering must be reported to the nominated officer where the information arises in the course of our business.

The definition of money laundering for these purposes includes the three crimes noted above in category 1. In particular it should be appreciated that the crimes involving 'acquisition, use and possession' and 'concealing, etc'. can be committed by the perpetrator of the crime. A person guilty of theft or tax evasion will also have committed a money laundering offence if he or she is in possession of criminal property.

Note

The Court of Appeal's decision in *Bowman* v. *Fels* [2005] EWCA Civ 226 has made changes to the way in which the legislation is to be interpreted. First, generally speaking, the money laundering offences do not apply to most litigation (including consensual resolution of issues in a litigious context). Secondly, the interpretation of the word 'arrangement' (see 1(c) above) is restricted to the act of facilitation – preparatory acts which do not themselves assist in the acquisition, use, retention or control of criminal property will not give rise to liability. Thirdly, the Court of Appeal's decision has preserved the concept of legal professional privilege. If information is privileged we cannot disclose the information to SOCA unless a waiver of privilege is obtained.

You should continue to report to the practice's nominated officer any knowledge or suspicion, even if you believe *Bowman* v. *Fels* makes the report unnecessary. The nominated officer, with the assistance of others, will decide upon the impact of the judgment in *Bowman* v. *Fels*.

The danger signs to watch for

- **Unusual settlement requests:** Settlement by cash of any large transaction involving the purchase of property or other investment should give rise to caution. Payment by way of a third party cheque or money transfer where there is a variation between the account holder, the signatory and a prospective investor should give rise to additional enquiries.
- **Fictitious buyer:** Especially if the buyer is introduced to the practice by a third party (e.g. a broker or an estate agent) who is not well known to you. Beware of clients you never meet – they may be fictitious. Wherever a meeting with the client is not possible, special care is needed.
- **Unusual instructions:** Care should always be taken when dealing with a client who has no discernible reason for using the practice's services, e.g. clients with distant addresses who could find the same service nearer their home base; or clients whose requirements do not fit into the normal pattern of the practice's business and could be more easily serviced elsewhere. Similarly, care should be taken if you are instructed to remit the net proceeds of sale to the estate agent who was instructed.
- **Misrepresentation of the purchase price:** Make sure that the true cash price for a property which is to be actually paid is the price shown in the contract and the transfer, and is identical to the price shown in the mortgage instructions.
- **A deposit paid direct:** A deposit, perhaps exceeding the normal 10 per cent, paid direct, or said to be direct, to the seller should give rise to concern.
- **Incomplete contract documentation:** Contract documents not fully completed by the seller's representative, e.g. dates missing or the identity of the parties not fully described.
- **Changes in the purchase price:** Adjustments to the purchase price, particularly in high percentage mortgage cases, or allowances off the purchase price for, e.g. works to be carried out.

- **Unusual transactions:** Those which do not follow their normal course or the usual pattern of events.
- **Large sums of cash:** Always be cautious when requested to hold large sums of cash in a client account, either pending further instructions from the client or for no other purpose than for onward transmission to a third party. It is the practice's policy not to accept sums of cash in excess of £[*amount*] unless prior approval of the practice's nominated officer has been obtained.
- **The secretive client:** A personal client who is reluctant to provide details of his or her identity. Be particularly cautious about the client you do not meet in person.
- **Suspect territory:** Caution should be exercised whenever a client is introduced by an overseas bank, other investor or third party based in countries where production of drugs or drug trafficking may be prevalent.
- **Mortgage fraud:** It is possible that a member of staff may unwittingly assist in a mortgage fraud. This is especially true of staff who deal with any form of conveyancing, whether domestic or commercial. We must therefore be very vigilant to protect our mortgagee clients and ourselves. If you turn a blind eye to any form of dishonesty over mortgages, no matter how small, you could be personally implicated in the fraud. It is important to stress that the penalties are criminal as well as civil.

Identification: general points

- In the light of the requirements contained in the Money Laundering Regulations 2007 it is the practice's policy to verify the identity of all new clients and all existing clients at the start of a new matter unless they have been identified already.
- Documentary evidence must be obtained in accordance with the procedure set out below. It is important that the original of any document is examined and copied. The fee-earner should endorse the copy with the words 'original seen' followed by the fee-earner's signature.
- Particular care must be taken when acting on corporate and private client matters. The 2007 Regulations require the client's identity and, in specified circumstances, the identity of a 'beneficial owner' to be established.
  Where we have a corporate client, the beneficial owner is anyone who:

  - owns or controls (whether directly or indirectly, including through bearer shares) more than 25 per cent of the shares or voting rights in the body; or
  - otherwise exercises control over the management of the body.

  Where we are acting on the estate of a deceased person, the beneficial owner is the executor, original or by representation, or administrator for the time being of the deceased person. Where there is an ongoing trust after the estate ceases to be in administration, the beneficial owner of the trust must be identified and verified.
  Where we are acting on a trust administration the beneficial owner is:

- – An individual with a specified interest in at least 25 per cent of the capital of the trust property (specified interest means a vested interest which is in possession, in remainder or in reversion).
  - – The class of persons in whose main interest the trust is set up or operates.
  - – Any individual who controls the trust.
- The identification procedures must be carried out as soon as reasonably practicable after first contact is made between the practice and the client. It is not necessary for the practice to wait until the verification process is complete before commencing work for the client. However, if it proves impossible to satisfactorily complete the process we must cease to act for the client.
- No client money should be accepted from the client for payment into a client account until the verification process has been satisfactorily completed.
- A client identification form should be completed and kept on the file (see 2.16).
- The copy of evidence taken to confirm a client's identity must be kept for a period of five years after we have finished acting for the client.

Identification: procedures

The method for identifying clients will depend upon the type of client. The procedure below and the documentary evidence referred to are not to be taken as an exhaustive list of requirements. A judgement must be made as to whether alternative or additional information should be sought. If in doubt you should seek advice from the nominated officer.

Companies

In the case of a corporate client we need to be satisfied that the company exists and that we are dealing with that company. The existence of the company can be determined by making a company search which reveals the following information:

(a) name and registered address
(b) registered number
(c) list of directors
(d) members or shareholders
(e) nature of the company's business
(f) certificate of incorporation
(g) if a subsidiary, the name of the holding company.

In addition, evidence of the identity of beneficial owners should be obtained in accordance with the guidance outlined above.

Individuals

The following information should be obtained for individuals:

(a) full name
(b) current permanent address (including postcode)
(c) date of birth.

At least one document from each of the following lists should be produced:

List A (evidence of name and date of birth)

(i)   Current valid full passport
(ii)   National identity card or resident's permit
(iii) Current photocard driving licence
(iv)   Firearms certificate
(v)   State pension or benefit book
(vi)   HM Revenue & Customs tax notification

List B (evidence of address)

(i)   Home visit
(ii)   Electoral roll check
(iii) Recent utility or local authority council tax bill
(iv)   Recent bank/building society statement
(v)   Recent mortgage statement
(vi)   Current driving licence (not if used in List A)
(vii) Local council rent card or tenancy agreement

Where joint instructions are received, identification procedures should be applied to each client. If joint clients have the same name and address (e.g. spouses) the verification of the address for one client only is sufficient.

Trusts, nominees and fiduciaries

Where the trust is regulated by an independent public body (e.g. the Charities Commission) the evidence of the existence of the trust and the identity of the trustees should be sought from that body.

In other cases a certified copy of the trust (and the grant of probate or copy of the will creating the trust in the case of a deceased settlor) must be obtained. The trustees must also be identified in accordance with the procedures for individuals or companies noted above.

In addition, evidence of the identity of beneficial owners should be obtained in accordance with the guidance outlined above.

Clients where there is no face-to-face contact

Where contact with the client is not face-to face but by post or telephone, it is still necessary to obtain evidence of identity in accordance with the above procedures.

Such evidence can be produced by way of an original document or by way of a certified copy provided that the copy is certified by a reputable institution, such as a bank or firm of lawyers, who should verify the name used, the current permanent address and the client's signature. The name and address of the institution providing the certification should be noted and checked by reference to a professional directory.

Non-UK clients

Non-UK individual clients should produce passports or national identity cards together with separate evidence of the client's permanent address obtained from the best source available. PO Box numbers are not sufficient evidence of an address.

Non-UK corporate clients should produce equivalent information to that obtained by making a UK company search. The results of company searches made abroad will depend upon the filing requirements in the local jurisdiction.

If you are unable to obtain satisfactory evidence of identity in accordance with the above procedures you must contact the practice's nominated officer who will advise on any alternative steps which may be taken or consider whether instructions must be terminated.

Departmental instructions

[*If appropriate include under this heading typical circumstances where different departments of the practice might find themselves at risk.*]

Help

Money laundering is real and it will affect us. If you have any concerns regarding the practice's policy or your responsibilities contact [*name of nominated officer*].

Conclusion

To minimise the risks of liability:

- **Verify the identity and bona fides of your client:** Meet the client or clients where possible and get to know them.
- **Question unusual instructions:** Make sure that you discuss them fully with your client, and note all such discussions carefully on the file.
- **Discuss any aspects of the transaction which worry you with your client:** For example, if you suspect that your client may have submitted a false mortgage application or references, or if you know or suspect the lender's valuation exceeds the actual price paid, discuss this with your client and, if you believe they intend to proceed with a fraudulent application, you must refuse to continue to act for the buyer and the mortgagee.

- **Check that the true price is shown in all documentation:** Check that the actual price paid is stated in the contract, transfer and mortgage instructions. Ensure that your client understands that, where you are also acting for the lender, you will have to report all allowances and incentives to the mortgagee.
- **Do not witness pre-signed documentation:** No deed should be witnessed by a solicitor or staff member unless the person signing does so in the presence of a witness. If a deed is pre-signed, ensure that it is re-signed in the presence of a witness.
- **Verify signatures:** Consider whether signatures on all documents connected with a transaction should be examined and compared with signatures on any other documentation.
- **Make a company search:** Where a private company is the seller or the seller has purchased from a private company in the recent past and you suspect that there may be a connection between the company and the seller or the buyer which is being used for improper purposes, then consideration should be given to ascertain the names and addresses of the officers and shareholders which can then be compared with the names of those connected with the transaction and the seller and buyer.

2.16 Anti-money laundering – client identification form

> **Note:** This form provides a basic precedent for a client identification form. It should be developed to suit the needs of individual practices. Reference should be made to **2.15** and the Law Society's Practice Note: Anti-money Laundering.

✓ **Client name**

✓ **Date of birth**

✓ **Address**

✓ **Postcode**

Client no.

I certify that I have carried out the appropriate client verification procedures as follows:

Individuals (including partnerships and unincorporated businesses)   Tick ☐

Risk assessment

I have identified the risk assessment as:

- Normal   ☐

- Enhanced   ☐

If enhanced risk, indicate the reason (tick as appropriate):

- Non face-to-face contact   ☐

- Politically Exposed Person   ☐

- Other higher risk   ☐

Verification

I have obtained the client's/clients':

✓ (a) Full name
✓ (b) Current permanent address
✓ (c) Date of birth

by reference to at least one document from each of the following lists:

List A (evidence of name and date of birth)

(a) Current valid full passport ✓
(b) National identity card or resident's permit
(c) Current photocard driving licence ✓
(d) Firearms certificate ✓
(e) State pension or benefit book
(f) HM Revenue & Customs tax notification.

List B (evidence of address)

(a) Home visit
(b) Electoral roll check
(c) Recent utility or local authority council tax bill ✓
(d) Recent bank/building society statement
(e) Recent mortgage statement ✓
(f) Current driving licence (not if used in List A)
(g) Local council rent card or tenancy agreement.

Where enhanced risk is indicated the following additional steps have been taken (specify):

```


```

I confirm having seen the original documents and that any photograph of the client bore a good likeness to the client. A copy of each document is attached to this form.

Corporate	**Tick** ☐

Risk assessment

I have identified the risk assessment as:

- Simplified ☐

- Normal ☐

- Enhanced ☐

If enhanced risk, indicate the reason (tick as appropriate):

- Non face-to-face contact ☐

- Other higher risk ☐

Verification

Simplified

Where simplified customer due diligence applies I attach evidence of the fact the company is of a description within Regulation 13 of the Money Laundering Regulations 2007.

Normal and enhanced

I confirm that I have carried out a company search and attach a copy to this form.

Where beneficial owners have been identified, I have verified their identity in accordance with the procedures for individuals or companies noted above or I have obtained a verification certificate from the company. I attach a copy of each document/certificate to this form.

Where enhanced risk is indicated the following additional steps have been taken (specify):

Trusts, nominees and fiduciaries	Tick ☐

Risk assessment

I have identified the risk assessment as:

- Normal ☐

- Enhanced ☐

If enhanced risk, indicate the reason (tick as appropriate):

- Non face-to-face contact ☐

- Politically Exposed Person ☐

- Other higher risk ☐

Verification

I confirm that I have received a certified copy of the trust (and the grant of probate or copy of the will creating the trust in the case of a deceased settlor). The trustees have been identified in accordance with the procedures for individuals or companies noted above.

Where beneficial owners have been identified, I have verified their identity in accordance with the procedures for individuals or companies noted above or I have obtained a verification certificate from the trustees. I attach a copy of each document/certificate to this form.

Signed   Date

        (Fee-earner)

Where the client has been identified as a PEP the approval of a senior manager must be obtained. The senior manager should sign this form as an indication of approval.

Signed   Date

        (Senior manager)

2.17 Anti-money laundering – internal reporting form

(FOR INTERNAL USE ONLY)
THIS FORM MUST NOT BE PLACED ON CLIENT'S FILE

1.	Name of client(s) Aliases/trading names
2.	Address(es) (including postcode, telephone, fax, e-mail and contact name)
3.	Date of birth
4.	Summary of instructions
5.	Beneficial owner(s) (a) Name(s) of beneficial owner(s) (b) Address(es) of beneficial owner(s) (including postcode, telephone, fax, e-mail and contact name)
6.	Evidence of identity (attach)
7.	Value of transaction
8.	Name and address of introducer (if any)
9.	Is the client named above the person you know or suspect is involved in money laundering? YES/NO
10.	If your answer to 9 is NO (a) Name of person you know or suspect is involved in money laundering (b) Address of person you know or suspect is involved in money laundering

11.   **Source and destination of funds**
 	
    (a)   **Source of cash/bank/other securities**
 	
    (b)   **Destination**

12.   **The whereabouts of the laundered property**
13.   **If you are unable to answer 12, do you have information which might assist in identifying the whereabouts of the laundered property? If so, state this information**
14.   **Reason for suspicion**
15.   **Does legal professional privilege apply?**   YES/NO

16.   **If legal professional privilege does apply, is a waiver of privilege necessary?**
    YES/NO
 	
    If NO, give reasons

Signed   **Date**
To be completed by nominated officer only **Report to SOCA?** **YES/NO** **If NO, give reasons**
Date business completed   **Record destruction date**
(If a report has been made to SOCA this record must not be destroyed at the 'date of destruction' without first referring to SOCA.)

2.18 E-mail policy

Introduction

Increasingly, e-mails are now used as the routine method of correspondence. E-mail facilities, together with access to the Internet, are available to all personnel through the practice's computer network.

The overriding principle is that e-mails are to be controlled and processed to the same standards as for normal correspondence. Because e-mails, both received and sent, are processed on an individual personal computer, in the majority of instances without the knowledge of a supervising [partner/member/director], there must inevitably be a high degree of trust from everyone regarding the use of e-mails.

Personal e-mails

You are not allowed to send personal e-mails using [*practice name*]'s e-mail facilities. [Partner(s)/Member(s)/Directors(s)] reserve the right to be able to view everyone's e-mails. E-mail accounts should be as open and viewable as mail coming into or going out of the office.

Legal issues

- All e-mails from the practice can be construed as legally binding so it is important to be careful about the content of an e-mail.
- E-mails should not be defamatory, obscene or of a nature which could in any way bring the practice into disrepute.
- E-mails should be treated as correspondence of the practice and care should be taken to avoid negligent or misleading statements.
- It is particularly important to be aware that contracts can be concluded by e-mail and therefore to be careful of this in the same way that you are careful in concluding contracts by other means of correspondence.
- The giving of undertakings by e-mail must be authorised by a [partner/member/director].
- [*Practice name*] does not generally issue or accept proceedings by e-mail, but where an exception is made to this rule it must be authorised by a [partner/member/director].
- All requirements of the Solicitors Regulation Authority (SRA) in respect of information in e-mails must be met, including that e-mails must contain a list of [partner(s)/member(s)/director(s)] and the words 'regulated by the Solicitors Regulation Authority' and the practice's SRA number for each branch. This will be dealt with by [*job title(s)*], who will arrange for standard wording to appear at the bottom of all e-mails.

Incoming e-mails

- All incoming e-mails related to client work must be printed out and a hard copy placed on the appropriate client file. If case management software is used, e-mails can and should be attached using this software where possible.
- As appropriate, the fee-earner is to refer any message of substance to the supervising [partner/member/director], either by discussing the e-mail with the [partner/member/director] or by forwarding them a copy of the e-mail.
- Any suspicious or offensive messages received are to be referred immediately to a supervising [partner/member/director].
- It is possible to set up an e-mail account so it can be viewed by another person (usually the secretary). Permissions can be restricted so that the details can only be viewed, not amended. This is useful when a fee-earner goes on leave as it means their secretary can check/review e-mails from his or her own computer. Care should be taken as often sensitive material is sent between the [partner(s)/member(s)/director(s)] of the practice.
- If a fee-earner is away from his or her desk for half a day or more, the auto-office message should be set and the relevant secretary is to check for any e-mails received and refer messages to the supervising [partner/member/director].

Outgoing e-mails

- As appropriate, outgoing e-mails of substance must first be approved by the supervising [partner/member/director] before being transmitted.
- A printed copy of outgoing messages is to be placed on the relevant client file.
- No potentially offensive messages are to be sent. Defamation, harassment and breaches of the practice's discrimination policy are all potential risks. Beware of the temptation to send off a hasty message that, on reflection, would be unwise. If you are annoyed or offended by an action taken or a communication received, a good rule is to reply later or the next day; by allowing yourself a 'cooling off period' you can avoid putting yourself in the wrong.
- Always check attachments to make sure you are sending the correct draft. Be particularly wary of a draft that might have been amended without your knowledge by someone outside the practice (client, opponent or other). Where this is a risk, you should attach the document as a PDF which cannot be amended (contact the [job title] if you do not know how to do this). Letters can be scanned in using the scanning function on one of the many photocopiers around the office. Instruction on using these is given at induction.

E-mail attachments

E-mail attachment size is restricted to [specify]MB. Large e-mail attachments can block the e-mail system and cause unnecessary load on the system. E-mails leaving the system are restricted by the exchange server, and it is possible to restrict individual e-mail accounts. External systems will often impose their own maximum size, so large e-mail attachments should be broken into more manageable sizes. See 'E-mail security' below for precautions to take when opening e-mail attachments.

Monitoring of e-mail use

E-mails are monitored regularly by the [*job title*] and could be reviewed by a [partner/member/director] if brought to their attention. Disciplinary action in accordance with the practice's disciplinary procedures will be used in the event that any of the provisions in this policy with regard to e-mail use are breached. The policy will be part of the induction process and any new employee should read, understand and accept the procedure.

E-mail security

- [*Practice name*] has [*specify protection measures, e.g. anti-virus, malware, adware or spyware protection or URL filters*] in place and it is the responsibility of the [*job title*] to keep this up to date. It is important that everyone remains vigilant to the threat of viruses in e-mails and reports anything suspicious to the [*job title*] immediately.
- [*Practice name*] employs a firewall with restricted access to assist with protection of its computer system and its connections.
- [*Practice name*] does not use encryption and digital signatures at this stage.

Precautions

- Do not automatically open e-mail attachments – they may contain a virus.
- Virus-check any attachment if you are unsure.
- If the attachment is a document which contains macros, do not allow the macros to run. Macros can contain viruses. If the document will not open, go back to the sender and ask for it to be re-sent.
- If you receive a suspicious e-mail, for example, from an unidentifiable sender, especially with attachments, do not open it. Be particularly cautious if the e-mail is from a familiar source but there is no text in the message. In such circumstances, telephone the sender before opening the attachment to see if they have indeed sent a bona fide message to you. Alternatively, refer the issue to the [*job title*] or the supervising [partner/member/director]. Where there is still doubt, the message should be deleted without being opened.
- If in doubt about an e-mail, do not open it.

Deletion of e-mails

It is your individual responsibility to review all stored e-mails and delete those that are no longer required. Be aware that all incoming and outgoing e-mails on client matters must be regarded as normal correspondence and are therefore subject to the normal retention periods. Before deleting any e-mails, fee-earners should ensure that printed copies of e-mails and attachments, including draft documents, have been placed on the client file.

Remember that deleted e-mails are still actually stored on the system and could be accessed in future. Although such e-mails may not be easily accessible, they could be retrieved from back-up.

PART 3

Client care

3.1 Client care policy

> **Notes:** There are regulatory and best practice principles to consider in relation to client care. Rule 2 – Client Care of the Solicitors' Code of Conduct 2007 and the forthcoming outcomes-focused regulation (OFR) have significant focus on the impact of a practice's actions. Practices must invest time in identifying, implementing and reviewing their client care policy and approach.
>
> The person with responsibility for client care should be someone with appropriate experience, skills and authority to fulfil the role.

[*Practice name*] is committed to providing a quality service to all clients. The practice's services should be recognised as being expert, accurate and appropriate. The practice strives to ensure that its advice is cost effective and communicated in a manner that is appropriate for each client. The practice is also committed to providing a truly professional service: it seeks to act with integrity and strict confidentiality in all its dealings with clients.

Our client care policy describes what this commitment means in practice and what our clients can expect from us. We will endeavour to adhere to the principle of putting our clients first, thereby ensuring that service excellence is an integral part of the planning and delivery of all services to our clients.

In order to achieve client service excellence, [*practice name*] aims at all times to:

- provide clients with a high quality, professional and consistent service;
- act in accordance with the [Solicitors' Code of Conduct 2007] and other relevant regulatory requirements;
- act in a respectful and courteous manner in all dealings with clients;
- represent our clients' best interest;
- ensure all our staff fully understand and are committed to client care in all their interactions with clients;
- ensure we communicate effectively with our clients and with an agreed mode of communication upon request; and
- give clear legal advice.

At [*practice name*], we make sure that our clients receive a client care letter that fully explains the level of service they will receive. In addition, we will name the person responsible for individual matters, their position in the practice and their qualifications. The client care letter will give the name of the supervisor responsible for each matter, and the name of the person who is responsible for dealing with any complaints.

In order that we can continually improve our service, we actively encourage and value feedback from our clients. We will use various methods to elicit feedback, including client satisfaction surveys and post-matter questionnaires. In addition, we monitor and evaluate client complaints to identify and address shortcomings and failings in our standard of service. Such feedback is essential to help continually gauge client perceptions of our service.

[*Practice name*] has the above measures in place to ensure we achieve our goal of providing a quality service. This policy will be reviewed annually on [*date*] by [*name of member in senior management team*] as part of the annual review of client care and as part of the annual review of risk, both of which are in line with the Law Society's Conveyancing Quality Scheme (CQS) Core Practice Management Standards.

Competence

The practice will accept instructions only where it can meet its commitment to the provision of an expert and professional service to clients. Where instructions would be beyond the expertise or the capabilities of the practice they will be declined. In any cases of doubt as to the ability of the practice to act appropriately for the client, [*job title, e.g.* the head of the conveyancing department] should be consulted. The practice's professional indemnity cover is limited to [*PI limit*]. We will not accept instructions where the consideration exceeds £[*amount*] million.

Confidentiality

The practice is under a professional and legal obligation to keep details of clients' matters confidential. This obligation, however, is subject to a statutory exception, which may require a solicitor who knows or suspects that a transaction on behalf of a client may involve money laundering or terrorist financing to make a disclosure to the Serious Organised Crime Agency.

If the practice is required to make a disclosure in relation to a client matter, the practice may not be able to inform the client that a disclosure has been made. The practice may also have to cease acting in the client's matter for a period of time and may not be able to tell them the reasons for it.

Under the new Law Society Conveyancing Protocol we are required to make the transaction as transparent as possible and to share information with others to assist in the efficient management of each transaction or chain of transactions. Before doing so we must obtain the client's consent. If the client consents to the disclosure of information about the transaction, other transactions in the chain or any change in circumstances, this information should be disclosed. We should encourage clients to withhold the authority to disclose in exceptional circumstances only.

In most circumstances it will also be inappropriate to reveal that the practice is in receipt of instructions from any named client. If you are ever in doubt as to whether you should reveal whether the practice acts for a given client, or give out his, her or its address, check with a [partner/member/director]. Breaches of confidentiality could cause considerable problems for the practice and will be treated by the [partner(s)/member(s)/director(s)] as a serious disciplinary offence.

Confidentiality can be put into jeopardy by thoughtless conversations and quick meetings in the reception area. Client business should not be discussed in the reception area. Wherever possible, a client should be escorted into a meeting room when they come in to sign a document or bring papers in. What should be a short and uncomplicated visit can easily change if the client asks questions and they should be entitled to do so out of the earshot of other clients or visitors.

All staff should keep personal conversations in the reception area to a minimum. The impression gained by clients overhearing conversations in the reception area can be quite negative.

Commitment

Buying or selling property is recognised as being an extremely stressful time. All clients are entitled to expect a real commitment from the practice in handling their instructions, and for the practice to attach appropriate priority to their requirements. A professional service does not involve becoming emotional, and this should be borne in mind in wording correspondence. If it is necessary to issue a client's ultimatum, make sure it is clear that the practice is acting on the client's instructions.

Courtesy

All clients are entitled to be dealt with in a respectful and courteous manner. This will have many implications, from not keeping clients waiting in the reception area without explanation, to showing them the way to and from meeting rooms. Staff should also be courteous when communicating via telephone calls and e-mails, as well as showing genuine interest in the client's matter and any concerns about it. This can be done simply by the practice being seen to do its best to help them.

Dress and demeanour

It is important that the practice should project a sense of professionalism at all times, particularly in its dealings with clients. First impressions gained by clients do matter. Everybody should dress in a manner which is appropriate for their practice and respects the attire required by certain religions and/or beliefs.

Professionals should also try to conduct themselves in a way that will reassure clients and enhance the practice's commitment to client service. This can be achieved by appropriate behaviour both in and outside the office towards clients, business contacts, suppliers and other third parties. A positive, respectful and professional approach will have a significant impact on any client.

Fee-earner responsibilities

Fee-earners must take responsibility to:

- make a reservation as soon as possible when meeting rooms are required;
- ensure they meet clients from reception and show clients back to reception;
- ensure that clients are not kept waiting;
- ensure that clients are shown hospitality and are provided with appropriate refreshments (coffee, tea, biscuits, etc.);
- if there is a delay of more than 10 minutes, advise reception of the reasons for the delay and give a time estimate for when the client will be seen;
- inform their secretary (if any) of their whereabouts in the building;
- ensure that reception and their secretary (if any) are informed if they leave the premises other than at lunchtime, telling them when they are leaving the practice's office(s) and their expected time of return.

Receptionists' responsibilities

The reception area is our 'shop window' and is critical to the first impression that visitors will gain of the practice. Receptionists should take responsibility to ensure that:

- all visitors are greeted appropriately and advised of any current delay;
- the relevant member of staff is contacted immediately via phone;
- clients are escorted to the relevant meeting room, if appropriate;
- clients are provided with suitable refreshments;
- the reception area is clean and tidy;
- newspapers and magazines are up to date and are neatly arranged;
- the practice's publicity material is made available to clients and is kept in presentable condition, and that floral displays (if any) are fresh;
- any colleagues discussing inappropriate topics, e.g. a client matter, are advised to vacate the reception.

If there is a delay of over 10 minutes the receptionist should endeavour to:

- offer an apology to the client;
- phone the member of staff and request an update to inform clients;
- inform clients of the reasons for the delay and actions to remedy;
- escort clients to the relevant meeting room, if appropriate;
- provide clients with suitable refreshments.

If there is a delay of over 20 minutes the receptionist should:

- offer an apology to the client;
- phone the member of staff and advise that they, a member of their team or secretary are required to deal with the situation;
- suggest a different appointment time, or organise the fee-earner's secretary to do so, if directed to by a colleague.

Confirmation of instructions

The general rule is that at or near the outset of every matter the client should receive confirmation of:

- the name and status of the person acting, along with details of the principal [partner/member/director] responsible for the overall supervision of the matter (contained in the practice's initial opening letter for conveyancing, which should always be sent);
- a written estimate of costs and disbursements in the practice's standard form;
- the terms and conditions of business under which the practice acts in residential conveyancing instructions.

Client feedback

A client's experience can have a significant impact on a practice. It could result in repeat business or a positive referral to a prospective client. To help [*practice name*] continually improve its service, feedback from clients should be actively encouraged and valued. There are various methods to elicit feedback, including client satisfaction surveys and post-matter questionnaires. Which method is used will depend on what is most appropriate for the practice or the client. Feedback will be regularly reviewed and escalated to management level.

The practice should also monitor and evaluate client complaints to identify and address shortcomings and failings in its standard of service. Such feedback is essential to help continually gauge client perceptions of the practice.

Our client care policy and feedback is the responsibility of [*name of responsible person*] and will be reviewed at least annually in [*month*] by the senior management team as part of the annual review of risk and in accordance with our obligations under the Law Society's CQS requirements.

3.2 Client care letter – conveyancing

> **Notes:** Refer to the Law Society's Practice Note: Client Care Letters (September 2010) for the content of a client care letter and for sample terms and conditions of business.
>
> This suggested client care letter is by way of example only to show that it need not be a lengthy document. Practices must not rely upon it and must draft their own letter to ensure that they comply fully with the requirements of the SRA.

[Practice contact details]

[Name of client(s)]

[Client address]

[Date]

Our ref: *[practice ref]*
Your ref: *[client ref]*

Dear *[name of client(s) – insert all if more than one purchaser]*

Your purchase of [*address of property*]

Thank you for asking *[practice name]* to act for you in connection with your proposed purchase of *[address of property]*. This letter, and the accompanying terms and conditions of business, set out the basis under which *[practice name]* will carry out the work on your behalf.

Your instructions

You want to buy *[address]* for the agreed price of £*[amount]*, subject to contract, with the help of a loan from *[name of lender]*, and you have agreed that we shall also be advising *[name of lender]* in relation to the purchase.

Responsibility for your matter

My name is [*name*] and I am [*precise status*]. I shall be carrying out the work relating to your purchase. [[*Supervisor's name*] is the [*specify supervisor's role*] and is ultimately responsible for your matter and supervises this department.]

I can usually be contacted by telephone on [*number*] between [9.30 am and 5.30 pm] on weekdays. [*Name*] who is a [paralegal/assistant] will be able to help you with any queries if I am not available when you call.

Costs and expenses

We have agreed a fixed fee of £[*amount*] with you for completing your purchase. The work will consist of the following:

(a) investigating the title to the property, to include:

   (i) carrying out searches with respect to title and local government information for the property;
   (ii) reviewing replies given by the seller to pre-contract enquiries;

(b) negotiating a purchase contract;
(c) negotiating a transfer document;
(d) advising you in respect of your mortgage offer;
(e) preparing a report on title;
(f) proceeding to exchange of contracts and then completion of the purchase;
(g) transferring funds by telegraphic transfer to the seller's solicitors and for relevant taxes;
(h) calculating stamp duty land tax (SDLT) on the purchase and preparing and submitting to HM Revenue & Customs the appropriate SDLT forms; and
(i) registering the purchase and the mortgage at the Land Registry.

Our fees are:

Fixed purchase price	£
VAT	£
Telegraphic transfer fee	£
VAT	£
[*Practice name*] total fees	£

[The price has been calculated on the basis that [*specify assumptions, e.g.*]:

(a) the property is currently held under a single freehold title at the Land Registry with no title defects;
(b) one contract is submitted to one purchaser;
(c) the purchase will be on the basis of an unconditional contract and the property is acquired with vacant possession;
(d) completion takes place on the date agreed in the contract;
(e) [*any other assumptions or exclusions*].]

If it becomes apparent that there are unforeseen circumstances in connection with the purchase we may have to increase our charges, but if that is the case, I shall inform you before we incur any additional costs.

In addition, there are a number of expenses which have to be paid to third parties to enable us to complete your purchase. These charges must also be paid by you.

The other likely expenses are:

Search fees (estimate)	£
Land Registry fee	£
Stamp duty land tax	£
Total expenses	£

If we find that any additional expenses need to be incurred after we have considered the contract, searches and title documents, I shall let you know the reason for the extra expense, the likely amount, and when we shall need payment.

If, for any reason, we have to abort the transaction related to the purchase of your property, I will break the transaction down into stages and advise what percentage of the estimated fee will be charged at each stage.

When you need to pay

We shall have to pay the search fees listed above very shortly. Please therefore let me have a cheque for £[amount] made out to [practice name] to cover the cost of these as soon as possible to avoid any delay as we cannot send the searches until we receive this amount from you.

I shall send you a statement showing all the other amounts due, including our fees, shortly before completion.

Next steps

I have asked the seller's solicitors to let me have a draft contract and other papers relating to the title to the property. As soon as I receive these, I shall begin the requisite searches in respect of the property which I estimate will take [timeframe]. I shall write to you as soon as I have all the information, including your mortgage offer, and we can arrange a convenient appointment for you to call to discuss the contract and searches.

If everything is in order, we shall then be in a position to exchange contracts with the seller's solicitor, after which both you and the seller will be bound to proceed to complete the sale and purchase. A non-refundable deposit of £[amount] will be payable by you on exchange of contracts and I shall ask you to let me have this amount when we are ready to exchange. The timing of the exchange will also depend on when the seller is in a position to do so. When we exchange contracts we shall agree a mutually convenient date for completion, the day on which you gain possession of the house.

The balance of the purchase price, including our fees but excluding the amount of your mortgage loan from [*name of lender*], will have to be paid to us a few days before the completion date to allow us to have cleared funds for the completion.

I understand that you wish to complete the purchase by [*date*], and while we shall do our best to achieve this, our ability to do so may be affected by matters outside our control.

Money laundering requirements

The law requires solicitors, banks, building societies and others to obtain satisfactory evidence of the identity of their client and, at times, people related to the client or their matter. This is because solicitors who deal with money and property on behalf of their client can be used by criminals wanting to launder money.

In order to comply with the law on money laundering, we need to obtain evidence of your identity as soon as practicable, and in any event before we can proceed with your matter. To collect this evidence, our practice is to [*set out your standard practice, e.g.* take a photocopy of your original passport and a copy of a utility bill].

If you are unable to provide us with the specific identification requested, please contact our office as soon as possible so that we can discuss alternative ways to verify your identity.

Our service

[*Practice name*] is committed to high quality legal advice and client care. If you are unhappy about any aspect of the service you receive, or about the bill, please contact [*name*] on [*phone number*], via e-mail at [*e-mail*] or by post to our [*office name and address*].

We have a procedure in place which details how we handle complaints, available at [*details*]. If you are not satisfied with our handling of your complaint you can ask the Legal Ombudsman to consider the complaint. Normally, you will need to bring a complaint to the Legal Ombudsman within six months of receiving a final written response from us about your complaint.

The Legal Ombudsman can be contacted at PO Box 15870, Birmingham B30 9EB, or call 0300 555 0333.

You also have the right to object to the bill and apply for an assessment of the bill under Part III of the Solicitors Act 1974. The Legal Ombudsman may not deal with a complaint about the bill if you have applied to the court for an assessment of the bill.

Terms of business

I also enclose this practice's terms and conditions of business which contain further important information about the way in which we shall carry out the work we do for you. If you have any queries or want to discuss any term further, please do not hesitate to contact me.

Your continuing instructions in this matter will be taken as acceptance of these terms of business and the information in this letter. However, I also enclose a duplicate copy of this letter and the terms of business and shall be grateful if you will sign and return both to us in the enclosed stamped addressed envelope as soon as possible so that we have a clear record of the terms of our agreement.

Yours sincerely,

[*Signatory*]

3.3 Closing letter

[*Name of client(s)*]

[*Client address*]

[*Date*]

Our ref: [*practice ref*]

Your ref: [*client ref*]

Dear [*name of client(s) – insert all if more than one client*]

[*Name of matter*]

As you know we have now concluded the work in relation to [*specify and, if appropriate, outline all steps that have been taken with concluding results*].

- Outline any action the client may need to take in the future with time limits if applicable.
- Return any documents/papers that you have been holding on behalf of the client.
- Specify any documents you are to keep in safe custody for the client with details of where they will be held, how long they will be held for, a reference number and details of whom they should contact for retrieval.
- Specify any charges for retrieval.
- Enclose copies of any documents that the client may need for reference purposes, e.g. completed copy wills, leases, land/charge certificates, copy of court orders.
- Specify whereabouts of any documents which the client is not to receive, e.g. charge certificate.
- Confirm that you no longer hold any monies on behalf of the client.
- Explain why you are holding any monies, and that you will issue an annual reminder.
- Account for any interest on monies held on behalf of the client if appropriate.
- Enclose client feedback form if relevant with stamped addressed envelope.

It has been a pleasure to act on your behalf. I enclose a brochure about the other services that [*practice name*] offers and we look forward to being of service to you in the future.

Yours sincerely

[*Signatory*]

3.4 Standard terms and conditions of business for conveyancing clients

> **Note:** These 'terms and conditions of business' are intended as a resource to enable practices to select those which are applicable to the way in which they carry on business. Some practices may prefer to provide some of the information contained in an opening letter or in some other form of written communication. Many of the conditions are alternatives and practices will need to select those which are applicable to the way in which they operate.

PLEASE SIGN AND RETURN

[*Practice name*]
Terms and conditions of business – property transactions

We set out in this statement the basis on which we will provide our professional services.

We are [*practice name*]. You are the client.

We are authorised, unless otherwise agreed, to take such action as we think necessary to obtain the required result. We shall not refer to the client for specific instructions every time we take a step. If, therefore, there is a limit to what we are required to do, or a limit to expenditure, we must be notified of this in advance.

People responsible for your work

The client's matter will be dealt with by a [partner/member/director], assistant solicitor, legal executive or conveyancing executive. A letter at the outset will be sent to the client stating who is dealing with the matter and giving the name of the supervising [partner/member/director].

Sometimes, however, work will be delegated to another member of staff where we deem it appropriate to expedite matters or to minimise expense. All support staff are closely supervised and the practice takes complete responsibility for their work.

Charges and expenses

Our fees are based mainly on the time spent by the [partner(s)/member(s)/director(s)] and staff acting for our clients. This includes: time spent on interviews; drafting of documents; reading and research; preparing and working on papers and correspondence; telephone calls; and any time spent travelling or waiting while on clients' business.

In addition to measured periods of time for e.g. interviews, drafting, etc., we apply a minimum unit of six minutes to each letter and telephone call. Items of a 'routine' nature, e.g. telephone calls solely to make appointments, letters of acknowledgement, etc., are not normally charged for.

The time so recorded is costed according to a formula, which gives a charging rate or cost per hour for undertaking work on clients' behalf, according to the level of fee-earner allocated to the client's matter (the 'charging rate').

We will give you a written estimate of the probable cost of the transaction and also of all disbursements which we can reasonably foresee at the start of the transaction. We will notify you in writing if for any reason we feel it necessary to vary that estimate and will explain to you why we need to do so. Any additional work will be charged at an hourly rate of £[hourly rate].

We will add VAT to bills at the rate that applies when the work is done. At present, VAT is 20.00%.

VAT is payable on certain disbursements.

We have no obligation to pay disbursements unless the client has provided us with the funds for that purpose.

We shall require such a payment in advance of search fees and other costs.

Where, for any reason, a matter does not proceed to completion, we will be entitled to charge you for work done on a time spent basis and for expenses incurred. Property sales and purchases which fail to complete often involve as much work as those which reach completion. Any charge made will not exceed the amount of our estimate even if the time spent would justify a higher fee.

Payment arrangements

We will deliver a bill following the exchange of contracts and payment is required:

- on a purchase: prior to completion;
- on a sale: at completion. If sufficient funds are available on completion, and we have sent you a bill, we will deduct our charges and expenses from the funds;
- otherwise when an account is prepared and a detailed costs analysis is undertaken.

If a bill is delivered in a concessionary figure ('but say') and remains unpaid after one month we reserve the right to credit the account with the amount of the 'but say' bill and to render a full account for all work done on the basis of a detailed costs analysis.

We reserve the right at all times to suspend action on the client's matter if these arrangements have not been followed.

We may charge interest on unpaid bills from one month after delivery of the bill on a daily basis at the rate specified in the Late Payment of Commercial Debts (Rate of Interest) (No.3) Order 2002 currently 8% over Lloyds TSB Bank Plc's base rate.

Acts of Parliament and regulations give our clients procedures for challenging a solicitor's bill.

For non-contentious work (legal work which does not involve court proceedings, e.g. conveyancing and probate), sections 70, 71 and 72 of the Solicitors Act 1974 set out your rights in relation to having the bill assessed by the court.

If the whole of the bill has not been paid we are entitled to charge interest on the outstanding amount of the bill in accordance with article 5 of the Solicitors' (Non-Contentious Business) Remuneration Order 2009.

An application to the court must be made within one month of the delivery of the bill.

Interest payment

Any money received on behalf of clients will be held in our client account. Subject to certain minimum amounts and periods of time set out in the Solicitors' Accounts Rules 1998, interest will be calculated and paid to the client at the rate from time to time payable on [*name of bank*] Bank Plc's designated client accounts. The period for which interest will be paid will normally run from the date(s) on which funds are received by us until the date(s) of issue of any cheque(s) from our client account. We may ask the client to sign a separate letter of authority agreeing that we may retain the first £20 of each amount of interest as and when calculated to help us cover the administrative expenses of arranging these calculations and payments.

Where the client obtains borrowing from a lender in a property transaction, we will ask the lender to arrange that the loan cheque is received by us a minimum of four working days prior to the completion date. If the money can be sent by CHAPS, we will request that we receive it the day before completion. This will enable us to ensure that the necessary funds are available in time for completion. Such clients need to be aware that the lender may charge interest from the date of issue of their loan cheque or the transfer of the payment.

Communication between you and us

We will aim to communicate with clients by such method as they may request.

We do not accept service of documents by e-mail.

We may need to virus check discs or e-mail.

Unless instructed otherwise, we will communicate with others when appropriate by e-mail or fax but we cannot be responsible for the security of correspondence and documents sent by such media.

The Data Protection Act 1998 requires us to advise clients that their particulars are held on our database. We may, from time to time, use these details to send information which we think might be of interest to our clients. We do not make such information available to any other provider of products or services.

[Speaking to your lender

We are also acting for your proposed lender in this transaction. This means we have a duty to make full disclosure to the mortgagee of all relevant facts relating to you, your purchase and mortgage. That will include disclosure of any discrepancies between the mortgage application and information provided to us during the transaction and any cashback payments or discount schemes which a seller is providing you. If a conflict of interest arises, we must cease to act for you in this matter.]

Financial services and insurance contracts

We are [authorised by the Financial Services Authority in the conduct of investment business and] regulated by the Solicitors Regulation Authority. We also carry on insurance mediation activity which, broadly, is the advising on, selling and administration of insurance contracts.

[We are not authorised by the Financial Services Authority. We are, however, included on the register maintained by the Financial Services Authority so that we may carry on insurance mediation activity, which is broadly the advising on and selling and administration of insurance contracts. This part of our business, including arrangements for complaints or redress if something goes wrong, is regulated by the Solicitors Regulation Authority. The register can be accessed via the Financial Services Authority website at **www.fsa.gov.uk/register.**]

The Law Society is a designated professional body for the purposes of the Financial Services and Markets Act 2000, but responsibility for regulation and complaints handling has been separated from the Law Society's representative functions. The Solicitors Regulation Authority is the independent regulatory body of the Law Society. The Legal Ombudsman is the independent complaints handling body who will investigate any complaints made against solicitors.

After completing any work, we are entitled to keep all papers and documents while there is money owing to us for our charges and expenses.

Storage of papers and documents

Concluded files will [in our discretion] be stored [or committed to microfilm].

Where stored a file of papers is kept in storage for not less than six years. After that, storage is on the clear understanding that we have the right to destroy papers after such period as we consider reasonable or to make a charge for storage if we ask the clients to collect the papers and they fail to do so.

We will not destroy any documents such as wills, deeds, and other securities, which we have been asked to hold in safe custody. No charge will be made for such storage unless prior notice in writing is given of a charge to be made from a future date which may be specified in that notice.

If we retrieve papers or documents from storage in relation to continuing or new instructions to act, we will not normally charge for such retrieval. However, we will normally make a charge based on time spent for producing stored papers or documents to the client or to another party at the client's request.

Identity, disclosure and confidentiality of business

All advice given to clients is entirely confidential, but:

* Money laundering regulations may require disclosure of confidential information by law. Please note: that we accept no responsibility for any loss arising from compliance with the Money Laundering Provisions of the Proceeds of Crime Act 2002 and any amending legislation howsoever caused.
* The Solicitors Regulation Authority and other supervisory bodies may call for a file which is the subject of a complaint.
* A court order can compel disclosure of confidential material in certain circumstances.

As part of our continuing commitment to providing a high quality of service to all our clients, [*practice name*] maintains accreditation with the Law Society's Conveyancing Quality Scheme. The audit procedure laid down by this scheme may require examination of clients' confidential files from time to time under strictly controlled circumstances and only to duly appointed and qualified individuals. Acceptance of these terms and conditions by any client is deemed to include consent to such disclosure, which may be withdrawn by you in writing at any time.

The law now requires solicitors as well as banks, building societies and others to obtain satisfactory evidence of the identity of their client. This is because solicitors who deal with money and property on behalf of their client can be used by criminals wishing to launder money. In order to comply with the law on money laundering we will need to obtain evidence of your identity as soon as practicable.

Solicitors are under a professional and legal obligation to keep the affairs of the client confidential. This obligation, however, is subject to a statutory exception: recent legislation on money laundering and terrorist financing has placed solicitors under a legal duty in certain circumstances to disclose information to the Serious Organised Crime Agency. Where a solicitor knows or suspects that a transaction on behalf of a client involves money laundering, the solicitor may be required to make a money laundering disclosure.

If, while we are acting for you, it becomes necessary to make a money laundering disclosure, we may not be able to inform you that a disclosure has been made or of the reasons for it.

[*Practice name*]'s policy is only to accept cash up to £[*amount*]. If clients circumvent this policy by depositing cash direct with our bank we reserve the right to charge for any additional checks we deem necessary regarding the source of the funds.

Termination

Instructions may be terminated at any time. Termination of instructions must be in writing, to be effective.

We will be entitled to keep all papers and documents while there is money owing to us for our charges and expenses.

Under the Consumer Protection (Distance Selling) Regulations 2000, for some non-business instructions, the client may have the right to withdraw, without charge, within seven working days of the date on which we were asked to act. However, if we start work with consent of the client within that period, the client loses that right to withdraw. Acceptance of these terms and conditions of business will amount to such consent. If it is sought to withdraw instructions, notice should be given by telephone, e-mail or letter to the person named in these terms of business as being responsible for your work. The regulations require us to inform clients if the work involved is likely to take more than 30 days.

Limited companies

When accepting instructions to act on behalf of a limited company, we may require a director and/or controlling shareholder to sign a form of personal guarantee in respect of the charges and expenses of this practice. If such a request is refused, we will be entitled to stop acting and to require immediate payment of our charges on an hourly basis and expenses as set out earlier.

Tax and planning advice

Any work that we do for clients may involve tax implications or necessitate the consideration of tax planning strategies. Any responsibility to advise on the tax implications of a transaction that we are instructed to carry out, or the likelihood of them arising, cannot be implied and must be the subject of specific and express agreement.

We will not advise you on the planning implications of your proposed purchase unless specifically requested to do so by you in writing, otherwise than by reporting to you on any relevant information provided by the results of the 'local search'.

Complaints

Complaints will be dealt with under the following protocol.

In the event of a complaint, the client will raise the concern in the first place with the person dealing with the particular matter.

The client should then contact the supervising [partner/member/director], whose name will have been notified at the outset of the transaction.

The complaint should be put in writing explaining what action is requested.

If these steps do not resolve the problem our clients should contact the senior [partner/member/director], by telephoning or writing. [He/she] is [*name of senior partner/member/director*].

A full copy of the practice's complaints procedure is available on request.

If the complaint is still not resolved at the end of this complaints process you have the right to refer your complaint to the Legal Ombudsman at Legal Ombudsman, PO Box 15870, Birmingham B30 9EB; telephone: 0300 555 0333; website: **www. legalombudsman.org.uk**. Normally, you will need to bring a complaint to the Legal Ombudsman within six months of receiving a final written response from us about your complaint.

Referral arrangements

We may pay a referral fee for work to be referred to us. In such a situation we will inform you in writing and will tell you what fee we have paid. The advice which we give to you will be independent and we will treat you the same as any other client. You are free to raise questions on all aspects of the transaction and any information which you disclose to us will be treated as confidential and not disclosed to the referrer or to any other third party without your consent. We will not act for the referrer in connection with the same transaction in any way at all and you are under no obligation to instruct us in connection with the transaction.

Property disclaimers

We will not carry out a physical inspection of the property.

We will not advise on the valuation of the property nor the suitability of your mortgage nor any other financial arrangements.

We will not advise on environmental liabilities where we shall assume, unless you tell us in writing to the contrary, that you are making your own arrangements for any appropriate environmental survey or investigations. We may, however, need to obtain on behalf of your lender at your expense an environmental search.

Terms and conditions of business

If you require clarification on any of these points please do not hesitate to let us know.

Unless otherwise agreed, and subject to the application of then current hourly rates, these terms and conditions of business shall apply to any future instructions given to this practice.

Although continuing instructions in this matter will amount to an acceptance of these terms and conditions of business, it may not be possible for us to start work on the client's behalf until one copy of them has been returned to us for us to keep on our file.

Authorities

Where we are acting for more than one person we have an obligation to obtain instructions from each of them. This may be inconvenient for you and so to enable us to accept instructions from either of you on behalf of both, you are asked to sign the authority at the end of the enclosed copy of this form. We will then accept instructions from either of you on behalf of you both.

I/We confirm that I/We have read and understood, and I/We accept, these terms and conditions of business.

You may accept instructions from either one/any of us on behalf of us both/all of us in connection with all matters relating to our purchase/sale and to any related transaction.

I/We agree to our details being retained on a computer database.

I/We have read the above. I am/We are happy to give you the authorities requested and to instruct you to act for me/us on the terms set out.

Signed ....….................

Date ....….....................

3.5 Client survey

[*Practice name*] is committed to providing a professional and cost effective legal service.

Please take time to fill in this questionnaire. By filling in this questionnaire we hope to better understand the needs of our clients. We will use this information to help provide an even better service in the future.

1.	How satisfied were you with the overall serviced received from us?			
Extremely satisfied ☐	Satisfied ☐	Not satisfied ☐	Unsure ☐	
Please feel free to comment				

2.	Are you happy to use [*practice name*] again?
Yes ☐   No ☐
Please feel free to comment

3.	Are you happy to recommend [*practice name*]?
Yes ☐   No ☐
Please feel free to comment

4.	In general, how satisfied were you with the service you received from [*practice name*] in relation to:			
	Extremely satisfied	Satisfied	Not satisfied	Unsure
How quickly we replied to telephone calls	☐	☐	☐	☐
How quickly we replied to letters or e-mails	☐	☐	☐	☐
The level of service provided by your conveyancer overall	☐	☐	☐	☐

5.	What could we do to improve the service you received from us?
Please feel free to comment

3.6 Clients complaints policy

Our complaints policy

[*Practice name*] is committed to providing a high quality legal service to all our clients. When something goes wrong, we need you to tell us about it. This will help us to improve our standards.

Our complaints procedure

If you have a concern or a complaint, please contact us as soon as you are aware of the problem so this can be addressed. [*Insert contact details.*]

> **Note:** Practices may wish to provide clients with a copy of the 'Making a complaint' leaflet which is produced by the Legal Ombudsman.

What will happen next?

1. We will send you a letter acknowledging receipt of your complaint within five days of our receiving the complaint, enclosing a copy of this procedure. [*Consider format for those who are vulnerable or have disabilities.*]
2. We will then investigate your complaint. This will normally involve passing your complaint to our client care [partner/member/director], [*name*], who will review your matter file and speak to the member of staff who acted for you.
3. [*Name*] will then invite you to a meeting to discuss and, it is hoped, resolve your complaint. [She/he] will do this within 14 days of sending you the acknowledgement letter.
4. Within three days of the meeting, [*name*] will write to you to confirm what took place and any solutions [she/he] has agreed with you.
5. If you do not want a meeting or it is not possible, [*name*] will send you a detailed written reply to your complaint, including [his/her] suggestions for resolving the matter, within 21 days of sending you the acknowledgement letter.
6. At this stage, if you are still not satisfied, you should contact us again to explain why you remain unhappy with our response and we will review your comments. Depending on the matter we may at this stage arrange for another [partner/member/director] to review the decision.
7. We will write to you within 14 days of receiving your request for a review, confirming our final position on your complaint and explaining our reasons.

8. If you are still not satisfied, you can then contact the Legal Ombudsman at PO Box 15870, Birmingham B30 9EB or call 0300 555 0333 about your complaint. Any complaint to the Legal Ombudsman must usually be made within six months of your receiving a final written response from us regarding your complaint. The Legal Ombudsman has provided further guidance on its service at **www.legalombudsman.org.uk**.

If we have to change any of the timescales above, we will let you know and explain why.

PART 4

File and case management

4.1 Procedure for acceptance of new matters, allocation of work and file management

Client enquiries

Client enquiries about possible services are received:

- by telephone to the office;
- by telephone directly to an individual known to the client, potential client or referrer;
- by letter, fax or e-mail;
- by callers to the office.

It is essential that all enquiries as to whether the practice could or would be willing to act should be dealt with as quickly, efficiently and courteously as possible. Even if declining to act on this occasion, the practice has the opportunity to make a favourable impression for the next time.

The decision about whether to accept work or not should always be taken by a fee-earner and if necessary authorised by a [partner/member/director]. For areas of work that the practice does not undertake, secretaries and receptionists may refer the client elsewhere, taking into account any existing referral arrangements.

These are the required response times for all enquiries:

- Telephone – call back within two hours.
- E-mail – reply within two hours.
- Letter – respond on date of receipt.

If the fee-earner is unavailable or offsite, then an out-of-office assistant message for e-mails and phone calls should direct enquirers to someone who can provide a response in the matter.

Client and transaction details

It is important to always record clients' personal details accurately to ensure that names and addresses are recorded correctly on the practice's database and on documents and also to ensure that we are always writing to the correct address and using the correct name. Full names, addresses, postcodes, dates of birth and contact telephone numbers should always be recorded. New clients should always be asked to complete the full initial client instruction form. Existing clients may be asked to complete the form in respect of the transaction alone.

Allocation of new instructions

The head of the conveyancing department will be responsible for the allocation of new conveyancing instructions to conveyancers. Where conveyancers receive a direct referral or are instructed directly by a client, the conveyancer must assess the risk of the transaction both in terms of their own competency and also from an anti-money laundering and mortgage fraud viewpoint. Inexperienced staff should refer the assessment to a supervising [partner/member/director]. All conveyancers have an agreed list of competencies and may not deal with any transaction outside that list without the prior approval of and supervision by a conveyancing [partner/member/director].

Risk management

All fee-earners must assess the risk of matters at the outset, during the matter and at the end of the matter before it is archived. If the matter falls outside the fee-earner's competence or has an unusual feature about it which will make it a higher risk, then the matter should be discussed with the fee-earner's department supervisor or a conveyancing [partner/member/director].

Similarly, if a matter becomes higher risk during the transaction, the fee-earner's department supervisor should be notified and they will consider whether the matter has now become high risk, in which case a risk notice will be completed in the usual way. At the end of all matters, a file closure form should be completed and a concluding risk assessment needs to be undertaken (see below).

The risk of a matter should always be recorded on the case management system or on the data form in the usual way.

Conveyancing risks include:

- On a purchase:
  - Failure to spot and obtain an appropriate undertaking in respect of second or subsequent mortgages.
  - Failure to submit an SDLT return within 28 days of completion.
  - Failure to lodge the application for registration within the priority period given by an OS1/2 search.
  - Failure to complete before expiration of mortgage offer.
  - Failure to complete within six months of the date of a local search.
  - Failure to spot anti-money laundering or mortgage fraud warning signs.

- On a purchase by a company:
  - Failure to register a charge by the company with Companies House within 21 days.

- On a sale:
  - – Failure to notice and to pay off a second or subsequent mortgage.
  - – Failure to account accurately to the client.
  - – Failure to account to the correct client.

After a matter is finished there needs to be a concluding risk assessment. This is noted on the file closing sheet. If it is considered that the client could fairly complain about the service provided or make a claim, the fee-earner must complete a risk notice on the risk notice form and forward it to the person responsible for risk in the practice. On receipt of such a notice, a view will have to be taken as to whether the practice is required under the terms of its indemnity insurance contract to make a report.

Conflicts of interest

It is recognised that in any conveyancing transaction there is the potential for a conflict of interest between the seller and the buyer, but in reality such conflict is usually rare. Confirmation that a conflict has been considered should be recorded in accordance with the practice's procedures at the commencement of a matter.

Key dates

A key date is any date which if missed could give rise to a claim against or a loss by the practice. Recording key dates both on the matter file and in [*details of back-up system*] will reduce the risk of them being overlooked.

Key dates in conveyancing will include:

- Registration of a charge at Companies House within 21 days of creation of the charge.
- Submission of an SDLT return within 28 days of completion date.
- Registration of a purchase or new lease within the priority period conferred by a Land Registry search.
- Completion of a purchase within six months of the date of issue of a local authority search.
- Completion of a purchase within the life (usually six months) of a mortgage offer.

Key dates to be recorded using case management system:

- Application for registration of a charge at Companies House to be sent on the day of completion.
- SDLT return to be submitted online on the day of completion.
- Application for registration to be submitted on the day of completion.

The key dates diary system is as follows: automatic flagging of key dates by case management system to fee-earner in the first instance, and in the case of any further delay, to the department head. Any relevant action is to be taken and noted on the case management system to update and create a new key date. A central record of a fee-earner's key dates can be run off as a report from most case management systems, if required.

Undertakings

Under the Conveyancing Quality Scheme, no undertaking is to be given by any fee-earner without the prior approval and signature of a [partner/member/director], except for the routine undertaking given in the Law Society approved form to discharge a specified mortgage by reference to date and name of mortgage lender.

Estimate of costs

A full written estimate of costs and disbursements should be given to the client at the start of the transaction. This must be included in the initial client care letter.

Client due diligence

Client due diligence should be carried out before a business arrangement is entered into with the client. Proof of the client's identity should be obtained in accordance with the practice's anti-money laundering policy and the requirements (where applicable) of the CML or BSA. Information should be sought as to the source of funds which a client is using for the purchase of a property and appropriate documentary support should be obtained.

This type of due diligence is an ongoing obligation and any change in instructions, e.g. change of name of purchaser, different source of funds, change in purchase price, should prompt consideration as to whether further analysis is required.

4.2 Client instruction form

[Client or fee-earner reference]

Full name (include first names)	
Date of birth	
NI number	
Full name (include first names)	
Date of birth	
NI number	

Correspondence address	
Postcode	

Contact telephone numbers	Home	
	Work	
	Mobile	
E-mail address		

SALE

[Client or fee-earner reference]

Estate agent	
Address	
Telephone number	

Address of property to be sold	
Postcode	

Name of mortgage lender	
Address	
Mortgage account number(s)	
Sale price	

Location of title deeds (if no mortgage)	

Is the sale of your property dependent on the purchase of another?	

Is there any other information that we need to know?	

PURCHASE

[Client or fee-earner reference]

Estate agent	
Address	
Telephone number	

Address of property to be purchased	
Postcode	

Name of mortgage lender	
Address	
Amount of deposit available	
Account number(s)	
Purchase price	

Details of mortgage broker (if applicable)	
Who is arranging your buildings insurance?	

Is the purchase of your property dependent on the sale of another?	

Is there any other information that we need to know?	

I/we confirm that I/we wish you to deal with this transaction on my/our behalf.

[*Practice name*] is accredited as part of the Law Society's Conveyancing Quality Scheme. This is designed to improve transparency of transactions, raise service levels and provide better communication and a more efficient process. To achieve this [*practice name*] would like your authority to enable us to share information with other parties involved in this transaction and any related chain of transactions.

I/we agree/do not agree to you providing information to other parties in accordance with the Law Society Conveyancing Protocol.

Signed   Date

Signed   Date

4.3 Policy for the giving of undertakings

No undertaking is to be given by any fee-earner without the prior approval and signature of a [partner/member/director], except for the routine undertaking given in the Law Society approved form (*Conveyancing Handbook*, 18th edition) to discharge a specified mortgage by reference to date and name of mortgage lender. (See Form TA13.)

No such undertaking is to be given unless [*practice name*] has a written redemption statement from the mortgage lender and is satisfied that the proceeds of sale will be sufficient to discharge the mortgage in question.

Where there is a second or subsequent mortgage there is an increased risk of it being overlooked. A clear warning must be marked on the outside of the file and flagged in the practice's case management system to minimise such risk.

Commercial charges on residential properties are often 'all monies' charges and secure a client's total indebtedness to the lender. It is essential that no undertaking is given without clear written confirmation from the lender of the amount that they will require to remove the charge from the property being sold.

Case references

- *Angel Solicitors (a firm)* v. *Jenkins O'Dowd & Barth (a firm) & (1) Barclays Bank Plc (2) Close Brothers Limited (3) Ellenwell Properties Limited* [2009] EWHC 46 (Ch); [2009] 1 WLR 1220; [2009] PNLR 19
- *Clark & another* v. *Lucas Solicitors LLP* [2009] EWHC 1952 (Ch)
- *Thames Valley Housing Association Limited & others* v. *Elegant Homes (Guernsey) Limited & others* [2009] EWHC 2647 (Ch)

See also the SRA Warning Card on Undertakings.

4.4 SRA Warning Card on Undertakings

© The Law Society 2009. Last updated by the Solicitors Regulation Authority, April 2009.

The SRA takes breaches of undertakings very seriously.

Your obligations are set out in rules 1, 5.01 and 10.05 of the Solicitors' Code of Conduct 2007 and its guidance.

Many transactions depend on the use of undertakings enabling you to negotiate and conduct your client's business successfully.

Where you give an undertaking

Those placing reliance on it will expect you to fulfil it. Ensure your undertakings are:

- Specific
- Measurable
- Agreed
- Realistic
- Timed

A breach of undertaking can lead to a disciplinary finding and costs direction.

Undertakings you give are also summarily enforceable by the High Court. Be aware that you do not become exposed to a liability within the excess of your firm's insurance.

Where you accept an undertaking

Ensure that in doing so your client's position is protected and you are not exposed to a breach.

If you are a regulated person or firm

- Be clear about who can give undertakings.
- Ensure all staff understand they need your client's agreement.

- Be clear about how compliance will be monitored.
- Maintain a central record to ensure and monitor compliance.
- Prescribe the manner in which undertakings may be given.
- Prepare standard undertakings, where possible, with clear instructions that any departure be authorised in accordance with supervision and management responsibilities.
- Adopt a system that ensures terms are checked by another fee-earner.
- Confirm oral undertakings (given or received) in writing.
- Copy each undertaking and attach it to the relevant file; label the file itself.
- Ensure all staff understand the undertakings they give when using the Law Society's formulae for exchange of contracts and its code for completion by post.

To report to us on a confidential basis, contact our Fraud and Confidential Intelligence Bureau on 01926 439673 or 0845 850 0999 or email redalert@sra.org.uk.

For advice, contact our Professional Ethics helpline.

4.5 Risk notice

File	
Client matter number	
Fee-earner handling	

Stage of matter (summarise)

Nature of risk now arising

Action already taken to minimise risk

Action that you consider is now needed to minimise risk

Signed	Matter handler	Date
Signed	Department head	Date
Received	Risk [partner/member/director]	Date

4.6 File risk assessment and conflict of interests check form

Matter instruction form including ID, risk and conflict checks

Title Mr Mrs Miss Ms _____ (other)	ID seen passport driving licence utility bill other _____ (specify)		
Surname(s)			
Forenames (all)			
Date of birth (first named client first)	**Date of birth**		
Phone (day time)	**(other)**		
Address			
Town	**County**		
Postcode	**E-mail**		
Property description			
Matter type **Sale** ☐ **Purchase** ☐ **Linked** ☐ **Remortgage** ☐ **Other** (specify) ☐			
Private quote £	+ VAT/ distributions	**Money requested on account** £	
Total costs limit £		**Costs review limit** £	
Conflict check done ☐	**Risk assessment done** High (authorised)* ☐ *Risk notice completed ☐ Medium ☐ Low ☐		